Spring 2011

Dear José,

D1526711

To the first of many (☺) –

For all of your continued support throughout the years.

The Best of PANIC! – ¡En vivo from the East Village!

Volume One

A small token of my appreciation.

Always,

Published in the United States by:
Fireking Press
www.firekingpress.com
Info: firekingpress@yahoo.com

Book Cover Design: David Kay

First Edition.

ISBN # 978-1456343330

The Best of PANIC! – ¡En vivo from the East Village!

Volume One

TABLE OF CONTENTS

Introduction from the Editor:

I started organizing the *PANIC!* reading series in June 2008 because nobody—save for the lovely Rachel Kramer Bussel (hostess of the über-naughty *In the Flesh* erotica series) and the controversial and prolific Nuyorican poet Luis Chaluisan—accepted my material for their readings—and I was being published in top erotica volumes at the time. I in fact found more than a few cliquish doors slammed in my face, but no names, I promise.

On and on I went, suffering through one predictable reading after the next, trying to feel my way around the New York literary scene—after a seventeen-year hiatus from my native city and the neighborhoods in which I discovered underground art and music (and men who entertained mutual eye-gazing) in the 1980s.

It was my boyfriend John's idea, really: I had just been published in the Cleis Books volume *Best Gay Erotica 2008* with fellow New York City-based writers Sam J. Miller and Lee Houck, both of whom are included in this anthology as well.

It was Pride week. The bar Nowhere, where the readings take/took place, was programming a week of parties and events. Along with Pietro Scorsone, a fellow writer and musician, Sam, Lee and I set up a microphone and read to perhaps 15-20 friends and onlookers. A modest affair, but people loved it. They told me it was what the East Village needed in the wake of Dean Johnson's death and the closing of the Rapture Café.

Erotica. Bizarro. Horror. Edgy poetry. And unabashedly queer—radical even. One thing I knew was this: I wasn't going to feature hipsters and downtown "celebrities" who thought they could write, *let alone read* (or claimed that they were writers as a kind of self-appointed artistic badge)—I was going to introduce new and unknown voices I would scout out at other readings, online, and through friends: ambitious writers to present to whoever cared to listen. And so, *Freaks Read* (the original name of the series) was born.

In January 2009 I rechristened the series as *PANIC!*, partly because of the happy hour creatures that freaked out and left the bar in packs as soon as we writers took it over for two hours once a month (*oh no, it's them!*). As you might imagine, this happened on several occasions. And I say, *sometimes you have to take out the trash*.

Part of my mission with contributing to the ailing New York City underground is to smear countercultural/revolutionary values in the face of the drones that have gentrified our city, New York City—once perhaps the ultimate nexus of American avant-garde invention and artistic revolution. I'm not saying that *everyone* who has moved here since the Giuliani tidal wave falls into this unfortunate category, but it's a substantial majority—as I travel to many points in this city, in four boroughs on a regular basis, and eyewitness its massive makeover.

Tweaking that knob a notch or two higher: Forging the transformation of *PANIC!* to *HISPANIC PANIC!* (beginning January, 2011) will surely twist certain arms in our current political climate, and with the growing number of closeted—and not so closeted—political conservatives moving into the East Village and other neighborhoods from their vanilla origins. (Not to mention the racist "gays" amongst us who wear liberal and enlightened sheepskin costumes somewhat convincingly.)

I've had to blacklist not-so-fellow transplant "gays" who've found great pleasure in smearing Latinos, namely Puerto Ricans (and not just unsavory individuals), blatantly and to my face. But the fact remains: The New York Latino communities that spawned me and many of the writers

11

in this book have been here longer than they have and are more genuinely "New York" to me than they'll ever be.

Add to that the fierce gay rights and Mexico-USA border debates that have fueled the rising number of hate crimes hurled against both Latinos and queer people. This is where the fault-lines cross, creating a much more intense potential for charged and passionate writing and poetry performance—the intersection of being queer and Latino, which is anything but dull.

The pieces in this collection, whether by Latinos or not, whether subtle or obscene, take swipes at convention and the mainstream/status quo, at the notion of following rules *just because*; at the fear of questioning authority and surrendering freedom and identity in the wake of obscene materialism and the increasing class divide that has wedged a seemingly permanent crowbar into our city's cultural landscape. A chasm that keeps wreaking havoc on the working class—the class that keeps the city running and gives it its heart and soul.

I feel lucky to have worked with such extraordinary poets and literary artists who, quite honestly, donated these pieces so that I could make this volume happen—they deserve all the applause. I simply strove to curate a collection both diverse and concrete and wound up with much more than that. This is writing from the gut, whether crude or refined— and be warned, some of it might disturb.

As for renaming the reading series *HISPANIC PANIC!* and revamping its format yet again for 2011: This is where it was headed organically (breeze the Table of Contents and this should be obvious). As I began navigating New York's massive Latino spoken word and literary scene upon my haphazard return in 2006, I realized that this is where fiery underground/revolutionary values are *still alive*. Downtown New York is in an artistic/cultural crisis—it's been castrated. Plain and simple: The gentrification nation barks a lot, but doesn't quite know how to bite.

The brand of people—artists—that continues to refresh theater, nightclub, literary, and music movements has been pushed out and replaced with a well-heeled professional, techno-savvy consumer class (however dowdy or hip they may dress). And, they don't give a shit about cultural revolution! The system generally favors them, in fact.

So I've made a conscious effort to make *PANIC!* a combative affair and timeslot—a queer island of irreverence, freedom, carnality, cultura, color, and resistance. And since so many other downtown gay/queer reading series have cropped up since *PANIC!* was born, it was time to fine-tune the laser beam and create a "looking-glass" event where the racial/cultural minority becomes the majority, and where guests, including non-Latinos/Hispanics and non-queers, who are usually in the majority, will find themselves in the minority.

I'm quite aware that this has disappointed a few people—but being the odd guy out is good for writing! Comfort zones are dangerous for creativity, I think. I've participated as the only Latino at non-Latino-specific readings; I've read at an all-black PANIC! reading that I hosted; I've been asked by women's groups to read at feminist events—so what's the problem?

As intercultural exchange and the galvanizing of the LGBT movement change the ways in which households operate and neighborhoods function in New York City (and elsewhere), we ought to keep up with that as writers and cultural producers. I don't want to curate *just* a gay men's reading series, or *just* a Latino reading series, or a *strictly* LGBT-only event—I want revolution, period. And revolution comes in many forms and colors—on the street, on the page, in the mind, in the heart, in the government, and in the bedroom.

How else are we to imagine our future in a city whose Latino/Latin-American population weighs in at almost a third of its total? How long will it take mainstream America to realize that the Spanish-speaking history of North America is older than its English-speaking counterpart—and by well over a century? How else are we to awaken the mighty and sleeping dragon we will eventually refer to as "Nueva York"?

Charlie Vázquez
Brooklyn, New York
October, 2010

The Best of PANIC! – ¡En vivo from the East Village!

Volume One

Lee Houck

Lee Houck was born in Chattanooga, Tennessee, and now lives in Brooklyn, New York. His debut novel, *Yield*, was the winner of Project QueerLit 2008, and was published by Kensington Books in September 2010. His writing appears in numerous anthologies including three volumes of *Best Gay Erotica*, *From Boys to Men*, and the Australian art book *Hair*, and in two limited-edition chapbooks: *Collection* (essays, 2006) and *Warnings* (poems, 2009). Additionally, he has worked with Jennifer Miller's Circus Amok! for many, many seasons. Info: http://www.leehouck.com

Activate Profile

Daniel sat in the dark, his thighs hot from the laptop, his face bathed in a glowing blue wash. The light from the screen shone out into the room, which stretched the potted plants into indigo-hued shadows, and the vases were rimmed with a shiny sapphire lining. Lucy had retired to her guest room and Helena turned in right after dinner. Even Baroness, after spending an hour curled up on the floor alternately gazing into space and bathing herself, went to sleep with her mother, where she stretched out on the end of her bed.

His only company was—again—the elaborate witticisms found in Internet personal ads, so bloated with the enormous crush of irony. The system assumed that your match was already here waiting, somewhere, and the talent lied divining him out of the masses, sifting him from the chafe. Everyone was competing for companionship, buried in word games, completely devoid of the flesh, the scent—the real senses—and the elegant exchange of molecules that comes from a real touch. Daniel imagined thousands of people across the globe, hundreds of thousands maybe, all clicking away, listing preferences and statistics, uploading doctored photos. (And, frankly, obviously undoctored ones.) Fudge a little here and there, they'll never know. Invent the person someone wants to date. Yuck.

Nevertheless. Here he was.

Scrolling through the promises.

He filled out his own ad months earlier, unsure of what he wanted or expected, and so it sat for a while unseen, invisible to the website's users. *What do you look for in a partner?* A fair amount of distance. *List some of your hobbies or interests*: Watching billiards on television. Using too much conditioner. *What is your idea of the perfect date?* Not a lot of talking and a couple of magazines.

He wasn't that courageous.

Instead, Daniel filled the spaces with answers that seemed (to him, at least) to be sufficiently vague. A few general cultural benchmarks, which would help readers fit him into their own structure: He wrote that he read D.H. Lawrence, which was somewhat true (he had read D.H. Lawrence, but didn't necessarily consider himself a *reader* of D.H. Lawrence); he wrote that he listened to "all kinds of music," because people are too sensitive about music, and a list of specific bands or singers, even vague genres, could raise acres of red flags; and finally, that he liked "independent films with solid scripts" and occasionally enjoyed a "summertime blockbuster about saving the world while blowing things up." He also included some random obscurity, which he suspected could be read—if the reader were looking for such a thing—as interesting and original: He liked ping-pong and Strawberry Charleston Chews®. It was a precarious balance. So much engineering.

This time around he chose not to mention his condition.

Let the picture speak for itself? It was a gamble—tell people ahead of time that they'll be dating a monster and you can expect zero responses. And yet, if he failed to mention it upfront, people (at the very, very least) accused him of lying. Generalized congenital hypertrichosis. Daniel was so accustomed to the diagnosis he could toss the words out like a stale cup of coffee, shuttling them into (and quickly out of) conversation without even a blink. But the medical terms meant nothing in people's ears, *dog-faced boy* was what they recognized, and it better described what he was anyway. He preferred it, in some ways. Dog-faced boy was aggressive, slightly poetic, with allusions to the circus, to antique pageantry. "Believe-It-or-Not," he would say, like a punch line. Hypertrichosis sounded like an affliction, a weighty illness, like he was a victim of the plague.

It was the plague. Sometimes.

Unless, of course, the guy was looking for a purely sexual experience. But tricks were too easy to find. No connection, no future, and rarely a real interest in the now—it bored him. He knew the look, the second glances. The impossibility of what they see standing in front of them—a novelty, a gossipy story they can repeat at parties. They peeled off his shirt, realizing that the hair doesn't end at his chest, and doesn't stop as it crosses over his shoulders, spreading down his back and across his buttocks, thick and curled on the inside of his thighs. They made surprise-inflected moaning sounds, spoke in quiet sex-whispers about how they could feel every hair brushing against their body—as if that were an original observation, even though for most of them, it was. They imagined they were sleeping with an idea, a vessel for their fantasies, something out of porn brought to life. Men were glad to have sex with Daniel, but they couldn't see themselves being with him for any length of time, making their relationship public. Gay men were so often looking for their twin.

The first man he ever slept with was so normal that Danny felt almost embarrassed to think of him now—all the details were missing. He was an accountant maybe, or real estate lawyer, or some other kind of job—a real job—which people did during the day and walked away from, basically happy, at night. Home to their microwaves and skin care regimens, their worn weekend sneakers stacked in closets. He was handsome, but not in the way that Daniel preferred. Daniel preferred a face whose neutral look was sad, almost mournful, a face that suggested seriousness, an esoteric intelligence. And he wanted his smile to be like a young boy's, with long, graceful eyelashes and glittering eyes like hard candy. But Daniel couldn't even remember his name—perhaps he had unconsciously planned it that way. He remembered only the fumbling through each other's underwear, the silly bobbing erections, like dumb vegetables.

And, of course, the comforting sameness.

Daniel knew he was gay ever since he could remember, but here he was actually *being* gay, *with another man*, which was something else entirely.

But this was Northern California, and among the cliques of artists and other like-minded liberal do-gooders (and deadbeats) all the talk was of a fluid sexuality. Everyone told him he shouldn't limit himself, he shouldn't subscribe to a label. And so there had been a girl before that, a human litmus test—an unpopular, slightly chubby girl with a keen sense of humor—even though he knew he wasn't interested in her, not really. Not the way other boys were. There they were: her clothes mostly on, his off, praying that his body would do what it was supposed to, and then feeling surprised when it did. Every part of her was infuriatingly soft and smelled sweet, like the plum candy she was always chewing. Her fingernails were all different, painted with colored markers.

"People say you're gay," she said, after it was over.

The air left his chest, seized in his lungs like wet concrete, and the blood pulsed into his head. He wanted to lie, and (strangely) that impulse made him more ashamed than her accusation. "What if I am?" he said.

"Nothing," she said. "I just wanted to know." She paused. "For sure."

"I still like you," he fumbled, scratching for anything that would shrink the space between them. Chasms could open so easily.

"Everybody wanted me to tell them what you looked like without any clothes," she said. Daniel wanted to vomit. "It's okay," she said, "I'm not going to tell anyone." She didn't say anything else after that, but rather stared at the carpet, running a curl of hair through her fingers. Girls, he imagined, kept secrets.

Men, he learned later, had even more secrets.

Men were impenetrable, locked behind unscalable walls, chained inside cages they too many times did not even see. And yet they were infinitely sensitive. Their emotions were wrecked with the slightest word; the most unconscious of gestures—you could lose them and never know it. They required long cooling off periods, retained impermeable inner lives, and you were never getting the whole of them. Men, himself included, were fundamentally broken, as if there was a genetic flaw in the species.

He had tried this Internet game before, a year or two ago. Miserably.

The first person who responded to his ad thought the picture was a joke—Helena's shot of him lying in a hammock at Lucy's house—and inquired about how one might use Photoshop® to cover yourself in fur. Daniel erased the message. Another man describing himself as "thirty-ish," who, like him, chose not to include a photograph, wrote that he thought they shared similar interests and were looking for similar things. Wary as he was to this sort of come on—he didn't appreciate someone else's assumptions about whatever station he might be at in life—Daniel agreed to a phone call, and so the man talked on for nearly half an hour about his garden (not so boring) and television shows featuring starships (very boring.) He then suggested that perhaps they would make "fine mates"—his words exactly—because not only did he have a hairy back and therefore knew what it was like to be looked at strangely say, at the beach, or in the locker room, but he was born with one normal arm and the other "shriveled and child-like."

"Do you play tennis?" the man inquired.

It was just too creepy—the tiny arm curled around the racquet, launching a twisted backhand. "No," he said, "I don't play tennis." Something in his response was so blunt that the man was quiet for a moment, thanked him for the pleasant conversation and wished him the best of luck. Daniel heard the closing of the lines, the crackling of copper wire or whatever it was that sent telephone calls around the globe these days. Satellites, maybe. He sat in the chair (again) at his mother's house, having fucked up another one, wondering how far his voice had traveled through the cosmos before landing—so wrongly—upon the man's ears. He wasn't interested in the guy, but the failure still hurt.

The next message was someone claiming to know of an experimental treatment…and that was as far as Daniel read. He deleted it immediately.

Fags, confused by the notion that hairlessness equals purity, often misunderstood him. They misunderstood what sex with him was—they were limited by their fantasies. Since Daniel was for so many only an idea, a story to tell in a bar over beers, a notch in their headboard—it usually felt like they were sleeping with someone else. Both of them there in the bed together, but not much connecting the parties, save for body parts. And they often became distracted. With Daniel in bed, there is always a lot to look at.

He clicked through the pages, one after another. *Next, next, next,* he clicked, exploring the details of a few here and there. He picked them by their faces. Daniel was into faces the same way that other people were into dicks or asses—he could stare at them for hours if they pleased him. It wasn't about symmetry or classic looks, it was about

21

originality. He liked people who didn't look like anyone else. And in turn, of course, they would have to like that also.

There was one ad placed by a man in San Francisco—with graying hair and expensive glasses—who spoke of recently finding his true love on this very website, and so now his ad, naturally, was posted only to find platonic friends. There was a picture of him taken at a coffee shop reading the newspaper, posed but meant to look casual. There was a picture of him in a tuxedo, hugging a pink satin-dressed woman, whose face was blurred to conceal her identity. There was a more recent picture of him with his newfound companion lying in bed together, smiling, the sheets and their tan bodies dappled with sunlight. They were a pile of backs and elbows and shins.

Daniel had fits of violent, stomach-turning jealousy when he was confronted with people like that, those cherubic couples who seeped love from their pores like pink corn syrup candy. For whom everything had been decided, and was accepted. He wanted so much to be half of that couple spooning against each other, whispering sentences, sharing breath and secret nicknames. Making promises that you both keep. But he had to admit the truth—that he was fundamentally incapable of such behavior, and so how could he expect that of other people? He was not open and accessible; he was instead closed like a cupboard.

So, what was he left with? Inane messages from men in other cities, people so desperate that they cast their nets like indifferent fishermen— including the same message cut-and-pasted from the same man three times, like some kind of reflexive obsessive desperation. *Willing to relocate*, it said. *Looking for The One.* But there wasn't any *One.* There was only hard work and compromises, maybe luck throws something good your way, and you find some fleeting moments of joy. Even love. Maybe.

And then, of course, there were the busy, over-talkative, deformed tennis players.

Daniel clicked the button marked "Activate Profile."

He picked a stray hair from in between the K and L keys, blowing across the screen. Then he sat back into the couch, and waited.

22

Jimmy Lam

Dominican by birth and Caribbean by choice, Jimmy Lam writes poetry, short stories, memoirs, political and cultural analysis and essays. He studied at the Universidad Autónoma de Santo Domingo where he attended the schools of Medicine and Humanities and graduated with a B.A. in English and French. He completed an M.A. in International Relations at City College in 2007.

His writing has appeared in English and "Dominicanish" in Santo Domingo, in New York, and on the web in: *El Listín Diario*, *El Nuevo Diario*, *Colour Life Magazine*, *Vanity Fair*, *Village Voice*, *Siempre*, *Dominican Today* and Cielonaranja.com. Jimmy's essay "In Defense of Pleasure: Sensuality and Eroticism in Dominican Women Writers in the US" recently appeared at the Dominican National Book Fair, in the anthology *Mujeres de palabra*. His book *Sexile* is scheduled to appear in the spring of 2011.

After a long and difficult sexual exile in Montreal and Oxford he's now established in Jersey City, with his partner Oskar, and writes the interminable memoirs, *Neurosis of My Own*.

For Oskar

By the end of June
A river of aroused lava
Descended from the Chimborazo
Cauterizing the snow-like laser
Towards the Pacific Guayaquil
To harden his cradle of waves

The deluge of fire fell like a revolt
of the same gods
Who in passed times celebrated in the Andes
And managed to nurture his body
While resisting his Caribbean roots

Since he was never hung onto a cross
Or had to walk over burning sands
He arrived intact
And with the eagerness of Don Quixote
Turned into a modern Midas
To defy the emperors in their salons

His infinite search for perfection
Makes me question:
What does he find by looking at death on my face?
What is the reflection of my scars?

And in spite of all the warnings
I fall in love yet again with his strength
As ivy tying myself to his obelisk in total rapture
Or punctually reclining myself
For the glare of his scapulas
To blind me

But don't they say that love is blind?

Out of the Morning Blues

For Jason

Just out of the morning blues
And with the ring of the phone
Unexpectedly
Surprisingly
Another visit: Unannounced

It takes me three seconds
To pick up the rooms
Ensure some clean towels and soap are still in the shower
Lube in the drawer
The handcuffs and his other toys
On the bed.

It takes him months
To contribute his absolute body
An authentic irresistible offer.
In his flesh
That old flavor of youth
An ancient aroma of rivers buried in the skin
Electric currents lie under his arms

Lover Black Man
Black Man Lover
Man Lover Black
Lover Man Black

Black Man
With more than pillars in your temple
Black man of marble y azabache
Give me your wonderful bone spatula
Cuz I am ready to purge my sorrows

Let me purify myself before I drink you

Black Beloved Man
Placed
At the intersection of God and Eros
Tell me:
How do you want it today?
Where should I serve you my best?
At the top of the bed?
Or pleading on my knees?

Tell me
How should I wait for you to bleed in me?

In my half-cookie mentality
Imported with the rest
I brought
A fear
A tremor for what I don't understand
An unnatural trepidation
For all the hidden and the secret

I cannot swim out to sea
Nor can I empty the jar
I am very much still there
As I am in this struggle

So
I don't understand
Your silences
Your disappearances
Your absences
And then you return one day
Just like that
Out of the morning blues

Cristy C. Road

Cristy C. Road is a 27-year-old Cuban-American artist and writer. Blending social principles, sexual deviance, mental inadequacies, and social justice, she thrives to testify the beauty of the imperfect. Her obsession with making art accessible began when publishing *Green'Zine* in 1996, a fanzine entirely devoted to Green Day. Today, Road has moved onto illustrated novels, taking both writing and visual elements a step more seriously; her visual diagram of lifestyles and beliefs stay in tune to the zine's portrayal of living. In early 2006, Road released an anomalous illustrated storybook, entitled *Indestructible* (Microcosm Publishing).

Road has also recently completed a collection of postcards featuring art from 2001-2007, entitled *Distance Makes the Heart Grow Sick* (Microcosm Publishing). In 2008, Road released *Bad Habits* (Soft Skull Press), an illustrated love story about healing from abuse, reconnecting to your culture and sex organs, drugs, and acquiring telepathic connections to the destruction of New York City. Road is working on new art, local organizing, and her punk band The Homewreckers. She hibernates in Brooklyn, New York, with a short attention span and a killer gas problem. Info: http://croadcore.org

Cubana encendida

"Oh god, I didn't even recognize you without your dreadlocks!" I told Tony, as he stood in the kitchen at that party last week.

"Yeah, I didn't recognize you either! You look browner. It might be your hair or the chest tattoo," Tony responded, and his sentiments were ambiguous.

He hadn't seen me since I had (partly fuchsia) inch-long hair; pale, vintage glasses, a striped dress and colorful leggings. Last week I was wearing a t-shirt, twelve years' worth of tattoos I had waited to get till I turned 24, and my hair was about fourteen inches longer. I had also decided to grow out my eyebrows—once elegantly drawn on my face each morning for about eleven years.

Last week I was unclear as to whether Tony was hurt that I defined his persona through his latter hairpiece, and used watered-down racism as a defense, or if he really was just that much of a tactless asshole. While annoyed at his language, I was aware of my rejection, recollection, and reconnection to cultural representation. The interaction circulated through my thoughts for about twenty-four hours, until the day after, when I was hanging out with Corrine.

Thinking about Cuba, and thinking about the past, my blood coagulated, condemning the unnecessary distance between itself and its soil. Giving free-reign birth to anxiety, my blood spoke: *Fuck this shit,* I reiterated as I sat by Corrine on my tattered upholstery and flipped on a muted CNN, while Pink Floyd's *Dark Side of the Moon* played in the background. As we snickered at the synchronized intervals, we waited for the broadcast of Obama's speech on Cuban-American relations.

I wondered how a president's alternative take on a seemingly endless blockade will affect the minds of the conservative pockets of the Cuban-American community that is my home. I wondered if finally, both Cuban and U.S. governments would choose to break the silence that's severed the cultural ties between burgeoning Cuban-American generations and the Cuban people. I wondered if American television would even broadcast this sort of thing.

Miami, Florida, is my hometown. Although it was always a little difficult to fully identify with a society which measured prosperity on plasma television sets—as opposed to verbal, physical, and creative intimacy. Criticizing the often conservative, abstinence-only, hetero-normative agenda of many Cuban-Americans with a voice, I rebelled as a kid, and into adulthood.

I chose punk rock as my route to survival. Eventually, this survival challenged me; merengue, my mentality, and the plate of bistec empanizado that sat before me on the nights of my childhood, where I felt alive. I festered on an imaginary border.

I would hear of Cuba and its lack of television and brainwashed citizens adhering to Castro's Cuba, without the desire to flourish outside of the government's organized constraints. Those terrible, exiled, political prisoners, comuñanga, fastidious with no criticism of the life they know.

I would cover my ears at the sight of generalization and seek benediction: How do we hear the voice of the oppressed, whether they slave, starve, or strive in Cuba? How do we hear the people of a minefield where free speech is mostly alive in secrecy?

I would hear of Cuba from American tourists. About the people talking, eating, singing, gozando, loving, bailando, comiendo mierda; under the sparkling rays of a sun that only burned like that above the Caribbean Sea. Frankly, I would like to visit because three-quarters of my entire family resides on the island. Because the way I value these un-American pockets of radical literature and anti-oppression is not *communist*, but *Cuban*—pre-revolutionary, post-revolutionary, and eternally the core of *culture* rather than *government*. I do *not* want to visit and deny my financial investment in a bureaucratic tourist industry that devalues the interest of civilians, to later feed my fetish for anti-capitalism with un dedito parado and a sign on my forehead that says *I'm here to learn that another world is possible. I'm oppressed in America, but I could afford this plane ticket.*

Hell, I invest in cruel bullshit all the time. And how different is a plane ticket than a piece of plastic made in Cambodia? I believe the embargo accentuates unnecessary fear within the mind of my generation of Cuban-Americans. I don't support or understand enforcing a physical blockade between people and their country, in spite of the greater system's clashing financial systems. Yet still, for the sake of my relationship with the soil of the island itself, I am cubana. My culture requires more debate with value, than does any other form of consumption.

For me, it's a financial struggle as well as a mental struggle; toggling a slew of personal values involving blessings, mamá, abuelita, and where my money goes. I am a Miami Cuban, born and raised on seven or eight cross streets that injected cubanita encendida in my blood. However, I'm not about to mistake my vast criticisms of capitalism for ultimate sympathy for Fidel Castro's rendering of communism. I don't like any government, but I believe they can change. I would oblige to have a word or two with Fidelito about tortilleras, mariquitas, and revolution.

My conclusion is natural: I will not demonize, or romanticize, but just respect what my distant friends and relatives say: The soil is perfect to grow your own food in the backyard, whether or not it's illegal. We play music, dominoes, and makeshift games outside, despite age, and social persuasion. We are socialized to help one another, whether or not we believe the government has left us to mostly help ourselves. We make with what we have, whether or not we are angry.

With detailed oppositions and embraces aside, I find the brainchild of our recent American leaders horrifying. *Fuck a bunch of borders, I* always mumbled beneath my breath at the sight of any unlawful delegation. Strengthening borders between societies strengthens blind animosity. The heat penetrating mankind's impression of my family's home and culture was not brought forth by the Cuban people, but by dogmatic political priests—as most wars usually are. Priests of neo-totalitarianism and priests of Reaganomics—priests in the back of my fifth-grade class assuring me that Haitians did not deserve to be here like Cubans did because Natalia's papi said so.

Thus, the Cuban, Cuban-American, Afro-Cuban, straight, queer, feminist, capitalist, socialist, anarchist, Catholic, atheist, and Pinko populations of the world *now* base their take on the Cuban people through battles which seldom illustrate my *self*: My blood is thicker than soil.

I don't like lavishness and riches to the degree of our world's Trumps, ranches, and estates. I don't find the way vast capital is used to be intelligent, nor useful. I don't like the vast division that is so obvious in the fabric of planet Earth: first, second, third worlds. Because 2,010 years ago someone decided what prosperity meant. Someone who didn't have much to do, so they created Western religious sects, and thus, resulted social classes, organized titles for ways of being, and a take on society that suddenly placed the color of our flesh and the construction of our morals on a global caste system, which many *able-bodied men* gladly acted upon.

Humans were "disabled," as opposed to just different than whoever was deciding whatever. Ancient treaties that belittled the existence of indigenous cultures began a mass exodus through the ocean. Conquistadors were now missionaries and westernization was now freedom.

Eventually, the ancient story of Jesus was sold to a pale-faced conservative who would decide the future of the following 2,150 years. He fell madly in love with the state, the Federal Reserve, and the new definitions of genitalia, biology, mental security, ethnicity, skin color, right, and wrong. Humanity suffered and celebrated, using organized religion to both assist and attack. It spent thousands of years unlearning the damage and rejoiced at any reconnection to self.

Eventually I grew up and accepted that that's just what happened and life goes on with what we have and who we are. Everyone holds onto their battle tightly, whether the world around them is crumbling or feasting on their idea of *vitality*. I left Miami, and my idea of vitality grew dented as I settled into a comfort zone outside of my culture. Vitality was measured by how much of a feminist I was, how pink my hair was, how thin my eyebrows were, and how long I could stretch my English activist vocabulary; while drowning in an anarchist community that sometimes elevated adapted struggles such as veganism, while dismissing the struggles of women of color.

As a kid, it was my Latina accents that pissed off my Latino classmates, whose insults constructed my premature definition of "pretty." So I hated my bodily proportions for several years, shaved the center of my eyebrows, my sideburns, and cut off my hair because it was reseco. Cuban girls wanted lavish strands of straight, dark hair, supplemented by the renowned stylist Mirta De Perales, who always encouraged blow-drying.

I only liked my hair when it was dirty. Greasy, tame, naturally gelled, but it was easiest to cut it all off. Assimilation was common sense to some—sometimes a regret to me. My reconnection to self is still in progress, but happened once I basked in who I was, and bolstered a sense of pride unheard of in my adolescence. I don't feel regretful of who I have been and understand it's nobody's fault for misinterpreting my ethnicity.

I don't think that's evil—I see evil behind dismissal of culture, color-blindness, and unnecessary woes for feeling *too white*. What's a woe was rejecting the parts of my culture that made me strong, because I found something bigger made me weak. I learned the Cuban right shackled me, as it repressed my desires to be myself, cubana, and a member of my family with pride I had lost.

Now, I'm a Latina before I'm an anarchist. I'm a starved cubichona salivating over the food and music my culture owns, before I'm anything—because I live in "America" and because I come from a line of diligent and overworked mothers and sisters. Because it takes work to live a genuinely cruelty free lifestyle, where internalized racism dwindles above all the morals we're trying to deconstruct.

I tell myself people undergo this work eternally, so I nitpick at the fabric of my world and myself until I feel safe, until I feel sane. I choose my friends and community with a new understanding; without a feeling silenced by the conservative paradigms of Miami, where it wasn't always safe to be queer or angry.

As Corrine and I awaited the broadcast, the same bulletin aired on heavy rotation. *At the recent Summit of the Americas, President Obama spoke of mending relations with Cuba and possibly lifting the travel ban*—a poised woman's voice would say, as they showed Obama behind a podium, lips in motion, yet inaudible. She reminded me of the announcer on the train during a delay. Every five minutes you think she is going to tell you everything you have waited to hear your entire life, but instead she just repeats herself, as the monotony pisses into your ear and you either get off the train or change the channel. We changed the channel; then we turned the TV off.

Dan Lopez

Dan Lopez is a graduate of the creative writing program at the University of Central Florida and a past Associate Artist in Residence at the Atlantic Center for the Arts where he worked alongside poet and novelist Sapphire. His work has most recently appeared in *Ducts, Prick of the Spindle* and *Time Out New York*. The story in this anthology appeared in the Fall 2010 issue of *Mary Literary Quarterly*. He currently lives in Brooklyn.

The Cruise

Despite the evening chill, he worked barefoot wearing only a linen guayabera and a threadbare pair of paint-speckled jeans. We'd seen him before tending to various small projects on deck, but it wasn't till Rogelio saw him on the *Patria's* aft deck repairing a loose railing that he became alloyed with a fervent sexual mystique in our collective conscious.

It began with those jeans. They seemed an odd choice for work pants. They were of a style recently fashionable, and they bore no obvious defects or stains beyond those associated with his work, which would justify so early a transition to a utilitarian role. No doubt they'd served another, more glamorous purpose not so long ago, and much thought was given to imagining that carefree life.

Specifically, we imagined what lay beneath those jeans, and, in cruder moments, how much semen had soaked into the fabric after bouts of reckless self-gratification or during fumbled adolescent attempts at coitus. The thought kept some of us sequestered in our cabins for days with dyspepsia, because even the best meals aboard the *Patria* were a bland substitute for the richness, we imagined, of his jism.

That first night, however, when we gathered to dance to all the songs that were popular on shore before we set sail, he had yet to come into his full erotic ascendency. Even Rogelio, so prone to theatrics, had little to say.

"Mind you," he said, pausing to light a cigarette.

"He's not *too* perfect. His nose is crooked and his ears stick out a little, but I wouldn't mind letting him into *my* aft cabin. *If* you know what I mean."

I was inclined to agree.

He had a face as smooth as milled lumber and the strong jaw of a boxer, which he was, and while his soft, boyish cheeks spoke to the ubiquitous desire within each of us to reclaim something of our misspent youth: he was not the type to merit more than a passing glance on shore. He was too short for that and his fingernails were always dirty from a variety of maintenance projects, and, of course, there was the nose and the ears to consider.

But, out here, he was something of a bright spot on an otherwise featureless ocean; a sort of erotic buoy we all used to track our position along a crowded shipping lane. He could be boastful in a way pleasantly at odds with his native fatalism, and his youthful stubbornness had a way of ameliorating into a sort of wounded dignity, which was centered in the darting passes of his deep-set, dark eyes. He had a pronounced Cupid's bow, which is to say, he had sexy lips, and he had a natural slimness, too, which, we would later learn, had more to do with a digestive sensitivity than with hours spent in the *Patria's* gym, and he had a wide, white grin, which emerged at the oddest of times, resulting in something of a parlor game to see who among us could produce the right blandishments to kedge it out.

The same tasks that left his long fingers coated in grease and perfumed with the musky scent of tar endowed his slight frame with a lean musculature that the guayabera did little to mask, and, perhaps, it was the irresistible cynosure of a body perfectly matched to its task that appealed to us the most.

Before long he came to inhabit a central role in our thoughts. We were envious of his rugged beauty and enthralled by his effortless adoption of life at sea. "*He* has a pert little ass," we would say to each other, in dispirited voices, as we toiled away in the *Patria's* gym. Or: "The salt does wonders for *his* hair. Why does it only dry mine out?"

In short, he became our primary gossip in a place when gossip was our chief diversion.

One day in particular, as we gathered to toast the sunset, Rogelio arrived out of breath and anguished over a fresh interaction. He immediately collapsed onto a chaise, his back to the sun and its predictable glory.

"There you are," I said. "We were afraid you were going to miss it."

"He spoke to me," he said, grabbing my arm, and it was all he could manage until someone brought him a drink from the bar. He took a long draft and only then did he begin to relax. The sunset passed unnoticed.

"I was up in the bow," he said, pressing the cool glass to his forehead, "sketching in my notebook when he sauntered right up to me. 'Excuse me,' he said, pointing a screwdriver at me. 'Can I squeeze behind you?' As you can imagine, I was nearly speechless. 'Claro,' I said, and stepped aside, motioning for him to pass.

He brushed by me and attended to something or other, and I was amazed at how little the wind bothered him. *I* was freezing, but he seemed fine in his guayabera. If it weren't for the line of goose bumps all along his neck you'd think it was ninety degrees.

"Well, I finally regained some composure and I asked him what he was working on. 'Boats like these,' he said, standing up. 'It's always something.' Then he slipped that screwdriver of his right into one of those pockets and smiled. That was it. That was all he said, but, santísimo, I could've died."

"You're so lucky," one of us said, and someone else added, "If it were me, I *would've* died."

Teófilo, who was principally known for his sublime ass and powerful thighs, and who suffered from a persistent yet mild seasickness, grunted. "You got to be kidding," he said.

"¿Eh," Marcelino said, "¿De qué se queja, Filo?"

"¿Esa?" Rogelio said, pinching a piece of lint off his trousers. "She's just jealous because she's never gotten into the spirit of *the cruise*."

"Coño, Filo," Marcelino said, "lighten up already, hombre!"

"I'll remind you," Teófilo said, returning to a chunk of spare wood he was carving into a whistle. "It was never my idea to come on this damn boat in the first place."

But we didn't want to hear that. We were in love; with the deep bronze of the boy's formidable neck, which only grew darker each day from the sun; with the chestnut hue of his large nipples, which always showed through the gossamer fabric of his shirts; with the smell of salt, which lingered in his wild mass of loose curls like sandalwood; with the way his long toes stretched across the teak deck or curled along the rungs of the guardrails as he scurried to replace a blown bulb. We were in love in a way we hadn't been in years on land, and despite whatever Filo thought, none of us was prepared to give that up.

We'd taken to lining the long promenade running fore and aft along the *Patria's* upper deck like two quivers lashed back to back in hopes that we'd run into him performing his duties. While the rest of the crew rotated throughout the ship, never spending more than a few days in any one spot, he was always on deck tending to minor repairs. It was as if having shipped an idol, the captain was at a loss as to what to do with him.

If we encountered him in his official uniform, however, the courtship followed a genteel etiquette. We'd greet him with a dissimulating nod, and he'd respond with a formal greeting and flash his mercurial smile, his thick lips sun-chapped and often cut from the blows he endured boxing the other crew below deck. If it was a warm day, he'd have a thin sheen of sweat on his brow, and he might brush a powerful forearm over the spot hastily so that we'd have to be quick if we wanted to see the dampness of his pits or peer beyond the strained cuff of his royal blue polo shirt into the dark hollow between his biceps and triceps.

Though we wanted nothing more than to line up like catamites ready to receive his large, uncut cock we always maintained a courtly distance when he was in uniform. We'd established a sort of gentleman's agreement about this. He'd indulge our lust on his off hours, and, in return, our erotic adventures would never trespass on the sphere of his assigned duties. Out here it was important to maintain delineation between the two worlds. We sensed as much early on, and we respected it, the restraint only adding to his erotic aura.

Only Teófilo, who even on shore was something of an iconoclast, ever violated the pact. It occurred during one of these formal exchanges on a day when the seasickness wasn't so bad.

"Muchacho," Filo asked, pointing a gnarled finger at the turbulent sky. It was in the hands that you saw Filo was older than he appeared. "What can you tell me about this weather?"

The boy, who had been replacing a broken hinge, stepped away from his work, crossed his arms and peered at the sky deep in thought. A moment later, he shook his head. "It doesn't look good, sir. Those clouds spell trouble, but it's nothing we can't handle."

"Hmm," Filo said, letting his hand drift toward the seat of the boy's khaki pants. "And the wind? Tell me, from which direction will it blow?" As he spoke, he pressed his hand against the rough fabric, caressing the gentle contours of the boy's ass. "These things affect me, you know. I have a grave sensitivity."

"I can't say," the boy replied.

"No?"

"No, I'm sorry, sir," he said and quickly returned to his work. "If you'll excuse me, I have a lot to do today."

"Of course," Filo grinned. "By all means continue. I've taken too much of your time already." He walked away, whistling, which is bad luck aboard a ship.

Filo never spoke of the boy again. When he would come up in our conversations, he would make a point of retiring to a corner to carve, complaining of queasiness.

If the hours of the boy's official duties were slave to a rigid etiquette, then the hours immediately following reveled in an equally immutable debauchery. It was then that we'd spot him barefoot on the deck in his guayabera and jeans. He'd chat with us, and, if he was in the mood, he would lay a hand on our shoulders, motioning for us to follow.

He'd conduct us to the bo'sun's locker on the crew deck. This was his refuge, the place where he housed his many tools and where he'd set up a small cot for the times when the idle chatter and stifling heat of the crew quarters proved overwhelming. It was here where we'd feel the roughness of those dirty hands as they tore at our throats and asses, making depositories of us for all his frustrations. He'd grab our cocks and if we felt fresh blisters as he stroked us, we'd know it had been a difficult day and we'd consider ourselves fortunate that he'd picked us out of everyone, and we'd brag about the savagery of the sex later that night on the dance floor.

We'd delight in depicting how he'd shoved us against the shelves so that our noses were buried in rags that smelled of camphor and tar, and of how he'd then taken a dollop of grease from one of the anonymous jars on the shelves and smeared it over our holes before he applied his stiff dick to our asses like a tool he was taking to some rough bit of line or a turnbuckle that had seized with rust. If you asked him to, he'd kiss you, and then you would taste the hot, sour dryness of his young mouth, and it would be the most passionate kiss of your life, but he never offered. For many of us, it was in that narrow locker where we learned that sometimes all we had to do was ask for what we wanted.

It was there one night, after he had finished with my body and I lay on the steel floor exhausted, content and slightly numb from whatever goop he'd purposed that he complained about the captain. "He's a bitch," he said. "He gives me only the most insignificant jobs."

I'd lit a joint, and offered him a drag, which he inhaled with conviction. "I didn't sign up to be a steward," he said, slamming the shelves with his palm so hard that the cans of epoxy rattled in their crate. "But," he added, a moment later, with a smirk, "I think I've finally convinced him. Tomorrow, they're sending me up the mast to adjust the radar."

"Congratulations," I said. "You deserve it."

"Yeah," he said, in a little voice. "You think so?"

"Of course I do. We all believe in you."

He stretched out along the cot. "I'm going to be captain of my own ship one day," he said, languidly slipping his big toe into my eager mouth. "A real grand sailing ship. Not like this piece of shit."

"Um-hmm."

As he spoke of his dreams, I alternated between massaging his calf and licking his insole.

He closed his eyes and took a deep puff off the joint. "You'll come, if you want to. So will all the others. There'll be room for anyone who wants to join me, and we'll travel everywhere—not just around and around the same dead piece of ocean," he sighed. "It'll be the most beautiful thing in the world."

"Sure, papi," I said, crawling up to his crotch.

If he ever completed the adjustments we never found out. Most likely he didn't. The following afternoon he got into a shouting match with the captain that ended with him storming the aft deck where we were marking time with coffee and a perpetual game of dominoes. He tore off his uniform, stripping to the waist with a wild, desperate yell, and we saw for the first time in the naked light of day the battered body we'd so willingly hitched our desires upon. All that we'd built up around him seemed to suddenly burn away in the bright light. He was just a boy, we realized, incapable of anything.

He climbed the railing and saluted us. "¡La Patria," he shouted, in a strained voice, "es la muerte!"

Then he threw himself overboard. It was a long time before anyone heard our pleas to stop the ship, and by the time the captain was convinced to hove-to and lower search boats into the water, he was gone. He'd often bragged about being a strong swimmer, and it was true that there were some islands not far off.

Perhaps, he swam to safety; perhaps, the sharks—there were many in that area—got to him first; or, perhaps, he stayed true to his word until the end and stubbornly drowned.

Either way, Rogelio, who had grabbed his waist in the final moment and tried to prevent him from jumping, held a vigil on the aft deck every night afterwards.

"He was going to get his own boat," he'd tell us when we asked how he was holding up. "He was going to take me with him—take us all with him. That was his dream."

We'd all been told one version or another of that same fantasy, and we'd all wanted to believe it—all of us except Filo.

Filo only laughed. "The only way that boy was ever going to get off this boat, compadre, was to jump, and if we were smart we'd jump too." Then he pulled his whistle out of his pocket and played a high note, which was bad luck aboard a ship.

Robert Vazquez-Pacheco

Robert Vazquez-Pacheco is a native Nuyorican gay writer and poet currently residing in Brooklyn. He is a former community activist, agitator, organizer and general agent provocateur. His work has been published in a variety of venues including scientific journals and fiction anthologies.

A Different Kind of Ghost Story

Given the mixed bag of experiences which constitute family gatherings, I can say there are very few family events I truly regret missing—but this one was definitely one of them. I don't remember why I wasn't there—I don't know why this wasn't a mandatory attendance occasion. Actually, it didn't start as a family event, and if you ask my mother and her sisters now, I'm sure they'd feign ignorance about it. It's that famously convenient family memory at work once again, you know the one. It remembers certain particular things, like how Cuca threw herself into her mother's coffin at the Ortiz Funeral Home, or how Hilda pulled a knife on her daughter Maria during an argument. The negative or embarrassing retain their freshness in the family's collective memory more than positive actions or triumphant moments. Memory is funny that way. I don't think this is unique to my family. Maybe it's just better to remember pain. You learn more from it than happiness.

I should start by saying that I come from a family of mediums and psychics. Everyone in my family has some kind of psychic ability. I grew up going to séances both at home and at relatives' homes on a regular basis. Spirit possession was a normal thing. Everyone had some kind of altar, the most elaborate belonging to my grandmother, who had a piece of built-in cabinetry for it. For me, ghost stories were not works of fiction. We are always surrounded by the dead. Ghostly messages and sightings were a regular thing for us. People, whether you liked them or not, never went away. There was never the concept of a final goodbye in my family.

Manuel, or should I say, "La Manny,"—if you know what I mean—was one of those old island queens, all long nails with clear nail polish, bay rum and guayabera, Brilliantined hair, thin moustache, bien pato viejo boricua. Un negro fino, which I have been called. He was one of those dapper old Puerto Rican queens and the expression is not meant disparagingly. He was effeminate but not feminine.

Although queeny, he embodied that walking contradiction of butchness and effeminacy that many Puerto Rican men have—that ambiguous machismo. *You know that you can fuck me, but don't kiss me because I am no faggot.* No homo. But Manny had to be strong. He and my grandmother both grew up in La Perla, reputedly the toughest slum in Puerto Rico.

A little about La Perla: La Perla was established in the late 19th century. Initially, the area was the site of a slaughterhouse because the law required them (and the homes of former slaves and homeless non-white servants)—as well as cemeteries—to be established away from the main community center; in this case, outside the city walls. Some time after, some farmers and workers started living around the slaughterhouse and established their houses there.

In spite of its oceanfront location (where in most cities such properties would be home to the wealthiest individuals), in recent years, La Perla has become better known for its high rate of illegal drug trafficking and crime.

Only three access points exist: one through the Santa María Magdalena Cemetery, one on the east side, and one through a walkway right in the center of the northern wall. Wandering into La Perla can be extremely dangerous for tourists, since their actions will be observed by locals from the moment they enter.

The thing I remember most about Manny though, what he was renowned for (within his various circles) both on the island and the mainland, was that he was a very fierce and powerful psychic, un espiritista. I'm also talking about the days before the psychic hotlines started, before Miss Cleo—even before Walter Mercado was on TV. Years ago, before John Edwards made it safe for white people, one could only talk about psychic stuff with family members, close friends and, sometimes other Latinos, and usually, in my experience, these people (at least all the psychics I knew) were always Puerto Rican. Or Cuban, because Cubans did the santero thing. White people were generally clueless.

As I said, everybody in my family was psychic to various degrees. For years I considered those abilities a kind of family trait, like light eyes or good hair. More likely it is an inheritance of the poor and powerless, that ability to have power in the spiritual world where one might be able to affect the world in ways outside of the material—how to have power if you are not white, rich, or male. Interestingly enough, in my experience, it was the women and the gay men who were the psychics.

Now, to make all of this even more interesting, I am the product of twelve years of Catholic education. I also spent most of my high school years on acid, but that is another story. But it was weird going to the strict all-boys Catholic schools on Mondays, listening to people talk about their various weekends, and realizing that yours were spent at séances and what are called "fiestas de santos," watching people caught up in spirit possession or sitting in the kitchen plucking the carcasses of various fowl killed in animal sacrifices. Humanely, of course.

That day, everybody (except me) was in Grandma's apartment in the projects. They were sitting around in her living room because the kitchen and dining room were too small to fit everybody—all were sweating because no one had air-conditioning yet. I don't remember if Grandma had plastic slip covers at the time or not.

Grandma was in her recliner, which was her throne. Manny was sitting in Grandma's rocking chair, the other seat of power. Grandma, whom I loved dearly, was once again holding forth about the good old days. You know how old people are. Sometimes it was great to hear the stories. Sometimes it was annoying.

This particular time, I don't know how they got on the topic, but Grandma started talking about how she never really got violent with her first husband, my grandfather, Domingo Pacheco. (Men in my family were always referred to by their full names. I don't know why that is, but my grandfather was always Domingo Pacheco. Occasionally he was "Mingolo," but generally he was always Domingo Pacheco. My grandmother's second husband was Luis Alvarez. My father was Juan Vazquez, my uncles Ivan Gallego, Joe DeJesus y Efrain Vasquez, my great grandfather Pepe Charleman. My godfather Donato Aviles. I don't think I'm referred to as Roberto Vazquez, probably more like "Papote.")

Of course, Grandma had the advantage of being able to rewrite ancient history because everyone else who was there was now dead and none of the kids were around. As she was sitting there reconstructing this history, Manny was sitting, rocking himself slowly in the rocking chair, drinking a Miller High Life®, fanning himself, listening to Grandma.

Then, imperceptibly, he slipped into a trance. Now, some psychics move in and out of trances quite easily. Some, like my aunt Hilda, make the transition more violently. In Manny's case, many times, it would happen when he was feeling relaxed and safe, especially around family. Here he was, having a brew and se le montó la negra. He goes into trance.

Everyone has a primary spirit guide. Manny's was a big strong black woman who'd been a slave, who wouldn't take shit from nobody, and was, let's just say, sometimes brutally honest. You know, a staple of the old telenovelas. Sadly, it's taken some Latinos years to finally dump that Aunt Jemima image. Manny went into trance and there went his spirit, who sat up straight. She leaned forward, looking right at Grandma, and said, "No seas tan paquetera, Provi." Don't bullshit us, Provi. She had called my grandmother on her bullshit story.

Everybody jumped up because they immediately recognized la negra's voice. "Oh shit," mumbled one of my aunts. My sister Elena, who was the person who told me this story, says she sat back, my sister that is, got comfortable and waited for the fun to begin. Cause nobody talked to Doña Provi like that, at least nobody alive. Spirits were something else. All the rules change for the dead.

Grandma said nothing. You didn't fuck with Manny's guardian spirit. The entity, using Manny, looked at my grandmother, called for a cigar and a glass of rum, and sat back. Then, smoking her cigar and drinking her rum, she related a story about how, when my grandmother was eight months pregnant with my mother, her fourth pregnancy, she came home one evening from work and found my grandpa, Domingo Pacheco, in bed with another man.

Can you imagine? (No, we don't know what he was doing and I've decided to not try imagining that.)

Well, my mother and my aunts were floored. After all, this was their father. My sister said she had to resist the urge to run to the phone and call me. Meanwhile the little kids were wondering what was happening and why did Aba look tense? *Aba, are you okay?*

Anyway, this former slave black woman spirit, embodied by Manny, sat back, puffing this cigar, drinking rum quietly. It was amazing how Manny's entire demeanor would change when he was possessed by this spirit. He got more butch—but butcher in the way that my great grandmothers or my grandmother were.

Then she proceeded to tell how my grandmother didn't say anything at the moment she found him. In bed. With another man. Instead, she cooked dinner like a good Latina and waited patiently until Grandpa went to bed.

Then when he was asleep, she climbed into bed, sat on his chest, belly and all, effectively pinning him down. She pulled out a big butcher knife (my aunt Milagros still has that knife) and placed it to his throat. She pulled out this major blade because she was going to slit his throat como un cerdo—like a fucking pig.

Needless to say, Grandpa freaked out and wrestled with her, eventually getting out of bed and out of the apartment. He was then chased naked into the streets of El Barrio, Spanish Harlem, in the middle of the night by his knife-wielding waddling pregnant wife who shrieked at him in Spanish.

And where did he go, like any good Puerto Rican man, product of the papi chulo syndrome that he was? A la casa de su mamá, of course. To his mom's house. His mom lived in the neighborhood, because back in the day, the entire family lived in the same neighborhood. So there was my grandpa, naked, screaming, and banging on his mother's door as my grandma, in her nightgown, waddled up the stairs after him, armed with a butcher knife.

Naturally, Abuela Pavi, my other great grandmother, let him in, leaving my grandmother in the hall. We never learned what happened next, although I know that they divorced two children after that.

Now, you can't refute the source. I mean this is information from beyond the grave. Literally.

My sister said you could hear a pin drop in that living room. Everyone was quiet as the subway rumbled by, my mother and her sisters shocked, and maybe even pained by this revelation about their father. Manny finally came out of his trance. He was annoyed and cursing at la negra, his spirit guide, for sneaking up on him. He was also totally unaware of what had just happened.

Unfortunately, no one could question him or even say anything to him since, in essence, he wasn't there. I mean he wasn't the one who told the story. Grandma knew better than to try to tangle with la negra and God help anyone who would try to elicit more information from her. My sister said she had *that look* on her face, the one that could strike you down at thirty paces. So nobody said anything, sort of changing the subject, and my grandmother went into the kitchen to cook. As far as I know, the subject was never discussed again, becoming one of the many not discussed family dramas.

But at first opportunity, when Grandma needed something from the store, my sister ran outside with my cousin Maria and they called me from a pay phone on the corner to tell me the chisme. Although I tried, sneakily I might add, to elicit more information from my relatives, nobody would talk. Needless to say, that was the last time, for a long time, that Grandma ever talked about the good old days. And poor Manny, may she rest in peace, never knew what happened.

Charlie Vázquez

Charlie Vázquez is a radical Bronx-bred writer of Cuban and Puerto Rican descent. His fiction and essays have been published in various anthologies, such as the iconoclastic volumes *Queer and Catholic* (Taylor & Francis, 2007) and *Best Gay Love Stories: NYC* (Alyson, 2006). His writing has also appeared in print and online publications such as *The Advocate, Chelsea Clinton News, New York Press, and Ganymede Journal.* Charlie hosts the monthly reading series HISPANIC PANIC! (formerly PANIC!), which focuses on cutting edge Latino fiction and poetry. He's a former contributor to the *Village Voice*'s Naked City blog and a retired experimental musician and photographer. His second novel *Contraband*, was published by Rebel Satori Press in spring 2010, and his third, *Corazón*, is wrapping up for future publication. He's also working on a short story collection and co-editing a gay Latino fiction anthology with novelist and cultural producer Charles Rice-González called *From Macho to Mariposa: New Gay Latino Fiction* (Lethe, 2011).

Madame Sonia's Little Mouse

It happened on either First or Second Avenue. I don't remember which because I never went back. It had been a rare day, a spectacular afternoon, and an enchanting evening—the western sky was red, green, and orange at sunset and the first slivers of night were blue and purple, far away in outer space. The dusking ceiling was slashed by a falling star that landed in the city surrounding me, within walking distance, or so it seemed. I walked toward it, toward that odd glow, realizing I hadn't had a single conversation in hours.

I was in lower Manhattan and no one spoke to me; no one projected their fear, need, or insanity onto me—a rare day in Gotham indeed. I walked beneath the somber pin-steeple Gothic towers of the financial district—their shadows long and fading into emptying streets, their gargoyles tired by the passing of sleepless decades, waiting for the moment when cruel gods would allow them to revel in mystical sleep.

I began my journey to the landed star and made my way through ginger-scented Chinatown, where little green turtles (as small as silver dollars) were sold by boys that held their hands out for money; where live fish squirmed on ice, attracting crowds of bickering women eager to cook them alive. I continued through the pulsing tenements of the Lower East Side, where I smelled pollo guisao brewing in more than one restaurant. "Tenemos especiales, papi," a brassy goddess said to me, as I stopped to take in the mambo aromas of the Caribbean, before making my way to 14th Street.

I passed a fortune teller's storefront—a large pane of glass with a small blue neon sign advertising FORTUNE $5. There was a large and baroque gold-framed mirror facing the street, so that the passerby could see himself; something about my reflection, my visage, was different. All was still inside and yearning to come to life; there were tasseled tapestries and landscape paintings hanging on the square walls. I noticed a small table topped with old cards and unlit candles of many sizes and colors—crystal balls and quartz pyramids.

While studying the small ornamented table, I noticed a young boy sitting at it. He was small and dark-haired—perhaps five years old. There was no one with him. He was swinging his legs off the edge of a crimson chair that dwarfed him; he waved at me, beckoning me to come in. I opened the door and asked him if he was okay.

"Yes," he said, his neck level with the tabletop, his elbows bent on the surface like broken wings.

"Are you lost?" I asked him.

"Have a seat." He was wearing a cartoon logo t-shirt and his lips and teeth were stained red from a frozen treat or juice. I sat, willing to be humored for a few dollars; mischief bloomed in my gut. "A basic reading costs five dollars," the little vampire informed me, his voice small and young like a songbird's.

I set a five-dollar bill on the table near his little hands, which he folded together in a knot.

As soon as I'd done this, his insect eyes locked with mine and his black eyebrows peaked into tiny wishbones. "What. Would. You. Like. To. Know?" he asked chillingly, with a deep voice that made my heart skip a beat.

I didn't know what to say at first. Leaning forward, I suggested, "Whatever it is that you see, of course."

"A longer reading costs more," he said with confidence, challenging me, putting pyramids and spheres and cards into a drawer.

"And how did you learn to do this?" I asked with mounting skepticism.

"Some people can do things *without* learning how," he declared condescendingly. He reached into the drawer and pulled out a pack of cigarettes and lit one with a tiny lighter. I expected him to cough with inexperience and was astonished by what happened next. "Now, what was your question?" he asked with stern authority, as lazy smoke curled around his little face. He let it seep from his mouth and nose like one of Godard's thieves; the cigarette out of proportion in his porcelain doll fingers.

Astonished, I took out a twenty-dollar bill and set it on top of the five—just to see what would unravel. *What to ask?* I searched through my thoughts and wishes and mysteries. As I was about to speak, he covered his ears and screamed, "Don't say it out loud—ask it to yourself and let me know when you're done!"

I hesitated in the miniature storm of his violence and touched my arm, to make sure I was there, to convince myself I wasn't dreaming. I followed his very specific directions and notified him.

He closed his eyes and began humming. After sneezing and using the tablecloth to wipe his nose, he rubbed his hands together, closed his eyes, and announced, "Your spirit needs to be cleaned. Because it is light, it attracts darkness that uses it for energy—you have a very serious problem."

A chill fell over me like a dark shadow, like a heavy theater curtain cut loose. Night had fallen and phantoms milled outside on the street, oblivious to my strange encounter. When I looked at the boy again, he seemed tinier and the room much larger; a cruel Hall of Mirrors hallucination was born in my mind, warping and squeezing and stretching; my eyes were fooling me. I wondered if I was being subjected to cruel ventriloquism—I'd never heard a child speak as such and never have again.

What is he doing now?

Standing on his chair with his arms stretched out at his sides, he announced, "He's here right now. He doesn't want to believe he's dead." He began crying and shaking and I wanted to end his spell and console him—no child so young should have to think about such things. Continuing, he said, "We will make him understand that he must leave now."

This has to stop.

His face contorted as if he were feeling pain deep in his doll-like body. Saliva ran down his chin, snot from his nose. "You must move on!" he shouted to the air, like a crazed carnival barker, plunging me into deep dread. "You must move on!"

Why isn't anyone noticing this?

My mousy host began to wail (AHHHH!) and when I moved forward to console him, he put his hand up to stop me—even though his eyes were closed and wet with tears. Struggling with his thoughts—as if arm-wrestling a giant in his mind—he lamented, "The spirit is lost and needs to leave, but won't. I have to try harder." Pulling the tablecloth away and holding it high like a petite matador, the boy said, "Put your forehead on the table."

I did as he asked.

He cracked an egg on the back of my head and began rubbing the slime into my hair, chanting in what sounded like Hebrew; his tiny fingernails and shell fragments scratched my scalp. He cut a lemon and squeezed each half over the pasty mess; my ears began to ring with savage abandon and I felt a tourniquet of pain twisting in my abdomen. Acidic vomit rose in my throat and stung my nasal cavities.

"Repeat after me, seven times," he demanded. *"Vagabond spirit be gone now—I know you not anyhow!"*

I repeated the incantation seven times and my nose burned even more, as if I'd inhaled water. He lifted my head up, put a towel around my neck to protect my clothes, and lit a small torch of bundled leaves. Blowing the blinding and bitter smoke onto me, he chanted, *"Be vanished for good and let him be—we shall restore his harmony!"*

The front door flew open.

A dark-haired woman in a red dress set grocery bags down and screamed, "Simon!"

Simon scurried away through a back door like a little mouse, gone in a second. Studying me, she exclaimed, "I'm so sorry...my son..."

"That's what I figured. Do you own this place?" I asked, embarrassed, trying to control the small and rushing cascades of slime running down my face.

"Yes, I'm *Madame Sonia*. I'm *so* sorry," the dark woman said, in a smoky accent that could've been French, Egyptian, even Hungarian.

I was taken by how beautiful she was. "It's not a problem—I just need to rinse my hair."

"Of course, follow me." She locked the front door and led me into a small apartment, through Simon's escape door, her gypsy hips swaying, her curvaceous torso twisting like a loose helix. On our way to the kitchen, we passed him as he watched cartoons on a couch; colors and shadows altered the features of his face. Clearing her sink with noisy bangles clanging on her wrists, she said, "He just turned six and thinks he knows everything."

While dunking my head into the sink and turning on the hot water, I said, "He may not know everything, but he knows quite a bit."

Spreading a radiant mother's smile, she said, "Oh, I know. But he never answers the question, sir."

Nathan James

Author and activist Nathan James, considered the "philosopher-prince of erotica" by reviewers, began his bibliography with the novel *The Devil's Details* (2005), the short stories in *Enchanted Morning* (Muscle Worshipers, STARbooks Press, 2006), and "Ten Days" (Love In A Lock Up, STARbooks Press, 2007). Nathan contributed to the Zane anthology *Flesh To Flesh* (Strebor/Simon & Schuster, 2008) with his story, *Thickness*. His novels *In His Court* (Forbidden Publications, 2006) and the critically-acclaimed *Check Ride* (Forbidden Publications, 2007) have enjoyed bestseller status.

Nathan was nominated by fellow authors in 2007 for the *Clik Magazine Awards*. He is a passionate activist, participating in the LGBT Steering Committee of the NYC Council, and speaking at antiwar protests and gay-rights rallies across the country. Nathan is a regular contributor to GBM TV, The Rainbow Collective, and The EDGE, where he writes articles of interest to the LGBT community of color.

In addition, Nathan does a political news segment on the popular LGBT radio broadcast, *Da Doo-Dirty Show*. A lifelong resident of New York City, Nathan's literary influences include E. Lynn Harris, James Baldwin, James Earl Hardy, Alexander Solzhenitsyn, Audre Lorde, and Herman Melville. Nathan encourages people to visit his website at www.authornathan.blogspot.com. He can be reached at nathanjames95@gmail.com

Thickness

Have you ever discovered something about yourself that excites and astonishes you at the same time? I'm talking about a moment when every neat, preconceived notion you've held in your life gets turned on its ear. Let me see if I can put it all together for you. My name is Brian Watkins, and the last couple of days of my life have defied all the nice little conventions I'd become so comfortable with.

Okay, I admit it, I'm still kind of young, only twenty-two, and I haven't begun to discover all of life's wonders yet. Well, let me dive right in. Two days ago, I was in my friend Manny's gym. Manny and I had been friends all our lives. Manny's dad had passed away a year ago, and now Manny owned the gym. It was late, and he was tired, so he tossed me the keys and told me to lock up the gym when I was done.

I was pleased to have some quiet workout time, and I was waiting on the last few patrons to leave, so I could do my reps in peace. I came out of the locker room, and there on the treadmill, was a man of about six-two. I'd never seen him in this gym before. He was bald-headed, with a neatly trimmed goatee, full lips, a wide, flat nose, deep-set brown eyes, and he was solid, thick, but not fat. He looked like he was in his early thirties. His caramel-hued skin shone in the bright white overhead lights as he ran, glistening with sweat. I watched his long powerful legs working as he jogged.

I was transfixed by his beauty, watching his graceful stride, even as I wondered about my strange attraction to this man. In contrast to him, I stood five-eight, with a close fade, thin mustache, medium lips, and a square chin. My dark brown skin showcased a ripped, worked-out body I was inordinately proud of. My body was solid muscle from my neck to my feet. I was hard, and I made the gym my second home to keep it that way. Biceps, pecs, delts, quads, glutes, lats, all were honed to what I felt were the best they could possibly be.

Naw, I couldn't possibly want this guy, could I? Yes, he was handsome, but I'd always thought big, thick men would turn me off. Too many muscle mags and muscle guys reinforced that notion in my head. Besides, he looked to be about ten years older than me, and I wasn't into older men...*was I?*

Being such a muscle freak, I'd never really given much thought to guys with other body types...until now. I watched as the man got off the treadmill and stretched out. Seeing him do that, did something to me. I felt that familiar stirring in my groin and hoped no one saw the embarrassing bulge in my shorts. The man, whose name I'd later learn was Rudy Nesbitt, started toward the locker room. He smiled as he passed me by the locker room door. *Why did I suddenly become weak in the knees?* Almost involuntarily, my legs took me into the locker room behind him. I pretended to look through my locker as I watched him undress out of the corner of my eye.

"Hey, man, could you pass me that towel?" His voice was rich, deep, and captivating.

"Sure," I said, passing him the towel from the bench. "By the way, my name is Brian. I'm in charge of the gym. I thought I knew everybody, but I've never seen you before."

"I'm Rudy. I just came in to check the place out. Somebody recommended it to me."

Rudy peeled off his T-shirt, revealing his big, beautiful body. Wide, strong shoulders. Massive, round pecs, with the most exquisite gold nip rings. Rudy was thick, with a gentle roundness to his belly that hinted of softness without being flabby. He had a deep navel that my tongue desperately wanted to probe. I watched him, trying not to let my jaw drop as he toweled sweat off.

"How—how do you like this place? Do we have a satisfied customer?"

"Yeah, you do," Rudy smiled, lighting up the room. "I think I'll join this place."

Oh, would you? What was going on with me? I've never been this awestruck by a guy, especially someone like Rudy, who I thought wasn't "my type." I'd always shied away from the thick "daddy" types, preferring the muscle men I usually hooked up with. But listening to Rudy's deep voice, watching him move with quiet confidence, feeling the power of him wash over me, well, this was *different.*

Rudy pulled his shorts off, and I thought I might faint right there. He had this big, round, perfect bubble ass. I was so hard by this time (and trying to hide it every which way I could) that I imagined my dick might just burst through my shorts. Rudy stood there naked in front of me, and I'm sure my eyes were as big as dinner plates. I tried not to gawk, but...

"Hey man, are you all right?"

"Umm, yeah, I kinda got distracted for a minute...I'm okay."

"Oh," Rudy chuckled softly. "Did I distract you?" *He winked at me playfully.*

Rudy walked off to the showers, leaving me speechless by my locker. My mind was screaming at me to strip and follow that gorgeous man into the shower, but there were a few other people still on the gym floor. Being caught ogling Rudy with a huge erection might be bad for me and the gym. So, with almost superhuman effort, I went back out to the desk, trying to will my dick down so I could work.

Within ten minutes, the other three patrons had finished their workouts, showered, dressed, and left. Rudy, however, was still in the locker room. I decided to check on him. I found him still in that hot, steamy shower, luxuriating as cascades of water rushed over him. Beads of water clung to his every curve, making me hungry for his sweet thickness. Almost on impulse, I ran out of the locker room, grabbed the gym keys off the front desk, *and locked the front doors.* I hurried back to the locker room, practically tearing my shorts and wife-beater off as I went, and strode into the shower. Rudy turned and smiled at me. Without a word, he stepped toward me, dripping wet, bare skin shimmering.

"Rudy, I...," I began.

"Shhh. Don't say a word," he whispered.

Rudy wrapped his big arms around me, and I could feel his long hardness against my six-pack. I pressed my own rock-solid dick against his thigh, and began to caress his shoulders. Rudy's torso slid wetly against mine as I let my hands explore his curves, and feel his softness. I couldn't stop myself. I kissed Rudy's neck, letting my tongue lap the beads of water from his skin. Rudy hugged me tightly, and his mammoth pecs felt so amazing against my smaller body. I writhed against him as he squeezed my ass, holding me in his meaty palms. I was getting weaker and weaker as Rudy drew me deeper into him: I began kissing his pecs, licking those sweet nips, flicking my tongue around those nip rings of his! I couldn't contain myself any longer.

"Rudy, oh, *yes*, man, Rudy, you're so awesome!"

"Go ahead, man." *Oh, that deep, sexy voice!* "Kiss me, man. Lick my body like I know you want to."

"Oh, *yes*, please, *yes*, I must…" My words failed me as I kissed Rudy's pecs and felt my knees giving way as I worked my way down his body, licking the roundness of his belly, probing that delectably deep navel, tickling Rudy's bushy black pubes.

On my knees now, with Rudy stroking my head gently, sensually, I licked his generous nine-inch shaft, which was, like the rest of Rudy, thick and meaty. Water dripped onto the tip of my tongue from the head of Rudy's dick, and that was it for me. Pursing my lips, I took him inside me, delicately at first, then plunging on in, feeling the fullness of him inside my mouth. I rolled my eyes upward as I serviced him, to gaze at Rudy's massive body towering over me. I flung one arm around his left thigh, and it was like holding onto a tree trunk. I held Rudy's dick in my other hand as I sucked him furiously, my head bobbing. I felt the clouds of steam around me, as I went on and on, thirstily drinking his pre-cum, as Rudy threw his head back, his hips gently thrusting as I worked his shaft. Just when I thought I was going to swallow pints of sweet Rudy-juice, Rudy gently guided my head away from him with those big hands of his. Pulling me back to my feet, we kissed fiercely, our tongues intertwining, hands ravishing one another.

Rudy broke away with a look resembling terror on his face and stepped back into the shower, rinsed himself off, and wordlessly, scurried off to the locker room. I sank to my knees again, wet, naked, weak, overwhelmed by the experience. I heard him dressing frantically, but I was too drained to pick myself off the wet tile floor and chase after him. Besides, the front door was locked. He'd need me to let him out. I sat on my bare bottom in the steamy shower, trying to compose myself. I was giddy, aroused, amazed and...scared. Rudy was so...big, so comforting, like the daddy-type he was, I felt secure in his arms...but what had I done to make him break away and dash off like a jack rabbit?

I heard him coming back toward the locker room. His footfalls were fast paced, angry (well, I did lock him in). Just as I was about to summon the strength to pull myself to my feet, Rudy came into the shower, his face showing annoyance. Damn, he was an imposing sight! Tall, stern, with a black Sean jacket, white dress shirt, deep blue Rocawear® jeans, black boots—and Nautica Navigator® watch—Rudy was a sight to behold. I sat there, still wet, small, naked and weak, and hoped he wasn't *too* pissed-off with me.

"You know the door is locked, right, man?" Rudy growled. *Uh-oh.*

"Y-yeah, Rudy. I'm sorry. Let me get dressed and I'll let you out."

"Why did you lock me in?"

"I didn't want anyone...to, you know, see us," I managed to say. "I wanted you so bad."

Rudy's expression softened a little. "I guess that makes sense. Sorry I snapped at you. Let me help you up." Rudy took my hand and effortlessly brought me to my feet. I felt so vulnerable standing there, bare and helpless, before this massively attractive hunk of a man.

"Rudy," I asked, "what happened? Did I do something wrong?"

"No, you didn't. Not at all. I think *I* did, though."

"*You* did? How?"

Instead of replying, Rudy walked out of the shower and sat on a bench in the locker room. I followed him and leaned against the wall. In spite of myself, I had no desire to cover up. I liked being naked in front of this man.

"Can I ask you something, Brian?"

"Of course."

"Are you a top or a bottom?"

"Well, I *prefer* being a top..."

"I'm a bottom. Always have been. But usually, everybody expects me to be a top. I thought you would, too, so I tried to leave before I…embarrassed myself."

Instantly my heart went out to Rudy. I understood exactly what he was getting at. Being big and thick, guys had automatically pegged him as a top. Rudy felt ashamed for being a bottom, which, in his mind, guys associated with smaller, weaker men than he. I was guilty of making assumptions, too. Rudy was not, as I mentioned before, "my usual type." I'd read all the "no fats, no fems" lines on the hook-up sites I visited; I'd bought into the negative stereotypes about "thick" men for quite a while. I was still surprised at the intensity of my attraction to him and felt a little ashamed at how long I'd held on to my preconceptions.

"Rudy, man, you have nothing to be upset about. You were incredible in the shower! I can't begin to thank you enough!"

"Thank me?"

"Yes! You set me free of my closed-minded ideas…about big guys like you."

"Oh, I did, huh?" Rudy allowed himself a little chuckle. It was good to see him smile again.

"If you're a bottom, Rudy," I leaned in close and whispered in his ear, "I can think of a few things I'd like to do with you…"

"Really?" He eyed my rising erection.

"More than you can imagine, man…really."

Rudy stood up and embraced me, and I could feel all his tension melt away. I held him for divinely long moments, savoring the feel of his leather coat against my bare skin. I breathed in deeply his scent, which was musky, yet sweet, and pressed my bare body tightly against him. We kissed passionately, this time with a tenderness I didn't fully expect. Rudy reached down and cupped my ass in his hands. He squeezed me, and as I gasped with pleasure, he gripped my thighs and picked me up off the floor. I wrapped my legs around his waist, and pressed my hardness against the contrasting softness of his abdomen. Rudy held me with ease, caressing my back and shoulders as I squeezed my legs around him.

I began humping Rudy's belly as he held me. Wildly, I kissed his neck again, sucking deeply this time.

"Oh, *yes*," Rudy moaned. "That feels *so* good."

"Rudy," I panted, "let me lick those gorgeous...nips, again, *please*..."

"Go for it, man."

I pulled my arms in toward me and unbuttoned Rudy's shirt. Exposing his chest, I went right to work on his right nip, feeling the roundness of it, and his massive pec on the tip of my tongue. I pulled at the ring on Rudy's left nip with my right hand, making him shudder with delight. I let my tongue dance on his nip, feeling Rudy's big body undulate in waves of pleasure. Finally, he let me down, and as I stood there, hot with anticipation, he threw his coat off and started to undress. I couldn't wait that long...I stepped up to him and unbuttoned the rest of his shirt. Just before I could undo his belt, Rudy bent over (*oh, that ass!*) and withdrew condoms and a smack packet of lube from his coat (I like a prepared man).

Handing them to me, I got myself together while he took off those tight jeans and let his boxer briefs fall to the floor. I pulled the rubber on (I'm well-endowed enough that I can see the lot number on a condom when I put one on) in breathless anticipation. Rudy embraced me again, and I felt his heavy breathing on my shoulder. Gently, I placed my hands on his hips and guided him to the space between the bench and the lockers. I stood up on the bench while Rudy spread-eagled himself, facing the lockers. I looked down at his beautiful, full butt, and marveled: *I want this...oh yes, I do SO want this!*

Have you ever been abreast of the moment, when all your ideas and thoughts about the way things are avail you nothing? Have you ever felt a sense of wonder at the newness of an experience that took your power of speech away? Can you fathom the cascade of ecstasy that accompanied that first, tenuous entry into a new sexual dimension? I was rushing headlong to that wonderful place as I knelt on the towel-covered bench and spread Rudy's cheeks apart. I let my tongue do the talking as I explored that soft man-hole, feeling its juicy wetness as I probed him. He jiggled with delight as I rolled my tongue against his walls and reached around his waist to stroke his diamond-hard erection. Rudy panted hard as I snaked my tongue deeper inside him; I felt my whole body tingle as he moaned and writhed under my ministrations.

Finally, I let my tongue find its way out of his hot, wet ass, slowly, teasingly, while Rudy gasped.

"Oh—oh—damn—man, please, please, *I want you inside me, please*...

"Rudy, your wish," I giggled, "is my command."

I stood up on the bench, got us both ready, and slowly, sweetly, advanced myself into Rudy's willing, quivering man-hole. I could feel him contracting himself as I plunged deeper and deeper inside. He tightened his walls around me, and *oh mercy that felt so good!* I began to work Rudy's ass, reveling in the feel of those huge cheeks slapping up against me, as I pumped furiously, and Rudy moaned, a single long utterance of total ecstasy that came from far within him. I had this big, strong, masculine hunk under my complete control as I rolled my hips in a grinding motion, making my dick hit Rudy's every pleasure spot. I bent forward and hugged him around his thick, soft waist. Pressing my chest against his massive back, I moved him around with my hips, letting my dick do this fantastically sensual slow roll inside his ass.

"Oh, Brian, don't stop, you're so good, don't *stop*...."

Rudy thrashed his head around wildly, as I kept at it, drilling him with an intensity I didn't know I could muster. All those "muscle gods" I thought were the height of sexual desirability faded away. Rudy was such a generous, enthusiastic lover!

I pulled down on his nip rings as I felt my climax coming, and I felt Rudy bucking and contracting, and...I came in a blasting release of rivers of come, filling Rudy up with my sweet white juice, just as Rudy shot his load onto the lockers in front of him. I held on to Rudy for dear life as the power of my orgasm threatened to sweep us both away...

Finally spent, drenched in sweat, Rudy hung limply in my arms. I guided him down to the bench, and straddled his waist to sit in his lap. We held each other, too overwhelmed to utter a sound. I looked into Rudy's eyes, and found there a profound relief, a gratitude that needed no words. He was also a kind, giving lover, something most of my muscle-bound lovers lacked. They, unlike Rudy, were too impressed with themselves. I was glad that Rudy had found in me, a partner who wanted him without judgment. I could see he'd been searching for this for quite a long time. I was happy we'd found each other, and was amazed at how, in so short a time, Rudy could lead me on such a journey of self-discovery.

"I guess we need to go back to the showers," I giggled.

"Yeah, we do," Rudy replied, affectionately kissing me on the forehead.

We showered together, lathering each other up, and admiring each other's bodies. We lingered under the warm water, in a wet, slippery embrace, then dried each other off and got dressed. Then we exchanged phone numbers and email addresses and made a dinner date for the next night. I let Rudy out, locked the gym up, and started for home.

I closed my eyes as I lay on my bed. I thought about Rudy and the ways we so arbitrarily put people into neat little places in our minds. As the breeze floated in through my window and caressed my naked body, I reflected on all the things Rudy had taught me today. I'd learned not to assume things about people based on their appearance. I'd discovered that bigness does not a top guy make. I'd been pleasantly surprised by the way I found big, thick Rudy to be so electrifyingly hot.

To think I'd let my head be filled up with all that "perfect body" garbage! There was softness, together with a strength and sweetness that defined Rudy, and made me want to rest my head for hours on his massive chest, and just listen to that deep, sexy voice. I imagined lying in Rudy's protective arms, feeling him against me, wrapping my legs around his massive thighs…and holding on to him, holding on, holding on, holding on.

The alarm hammered my ears and I bolted up in bed. Damn. Morning already! Well, it wasn't a bad thing, I mused. I'd awakened to a new day, my mind open to all its immense possibilities, unchained. Rudy had, with a "thickness," set me free. I couldn't wait to see what else he had to teach me.

Nívea Castro

Nívea Castro, a Nuyorican who recently returned to New York City, has been an LGBT womanist activist since coming out soon after Stonewall. She is a lawyer, educator, scuba diver, salsera, world traveler, and a newbie photographer. Nívea's latest project documents, with photos and the written word, Latina dykes' experiences throughout the Americas. Her writing has been in the legal field, short fiction, and now poetry for the spoken form.

Actions of a Household Item

I was never a vacuum cleaner
except for when
I
sucked,
snorted,
inhaled,
white powder
up one nostril then the other.

Neatly cut razor-sharp thin lines.
Taking turns with others of like craving.
Crammed in a bathroom stall or
huddled over whoever's coffee table.

My friends, not friends
taught me to roll the dollar bill,
making a show, creating the ritual, sampling,
declaring, *'dis is good shet.'*

Hit after hit of mind-numbing/instant confidence/
don't give a shit/because feeling grooved right now is all that matters.

I'm hooked.
Like a vacuum cleaner hanging in a closet.

Me gusta esta casa (I like this home)

My mother said those were my first words
My childhood verdict
Of our brand new public housing third floor three-bedroom apartment.
A step up from El Barrio's two-room tenement we left behind.

This was the home
Where she gave birth to her last child
And the first to die
from colon cancer
but that's another story.

This was the home
Where she dreamt and saved and begged
To move to Long Island
To a freestanding house in Babylon, preferably.
But my father said "No." He liked Brooklyn.

This was the home
Where her knock on the metallic style apartment door
Could bring trouble or joy
Depending on her mood
Or the type of day she had
After working brutal hours at her factory job.

This was the home
Where she would leave us at night with stern orders to
No le abra la puerta a nadie – don't open that door
Unless it was she knocking to come in.
I, her eldest and only daughter
Took charge, stood guard
When she was away.

This was the home
Where her baby at three
Learned to work open the door lock.
And nothing would stop him from breaching security
Until the day she laid in wait
And rapped un cocotazo on his tender head
with the heel of her hard sole shoe.

This *was* the *home*
She allowed her daughter
To bring home
The pastor's daughter
For overnight stays.

In the twin-sized bed
Where they sleep oh so close
they came to experiment
Belly to belly hush-hush sensations
Like shooting stars on a new moon night.

Smooth movements against each other's thighs
their natural syncopated rhythm created private dancers
un baile para salseras.

This was the home where *her man* left her
for a younger woman
in the same building up on the 12th floor.
His lover turned out to be the reason
he said
"NO….no muvin to Babalón."

In this home
She lost her laughter, her groove, her drive.
My mother did not curse
Her

mala suerte
because
her religion forbade speaking foul words.
Nor did she believe in bad luck.

But nothing
would stop her
from acting out on her children
with
belt buckled leather straps.
Spawning
chunks
of crisscrossed
bloody
welts.

Up, down, sideways
From neck
To thighs

Especially on the daughter
who loved
the pastor's daughter
more than her.

Dario Dalla Lasta

Dario Dalla Lasta is a graduate of Pepperdine University and Pepperdine University School of Law. On the roller coaster ride of his life so far, he's been a lawyer, a divorcee, a music industry pundit, an actor, a go-go boy, and a fetish model. For the past six years, he's been hitting the queer scene as DJ Dario Speedwagon, spinning "cock rock and pussy pop" throughout Brooklyn and New York City. "The Three Red Lines" is his first novel.

The Three Red Lines (novel excerpt)

Not knowing how long he'd been asleep or what he'd been dreaming beforehand, if anything, Walt suddenly found himself in a big house of sorts. He was being led down stairs and hallways, but it was difficult to see because something was over his head, like a bag or a bucket. He noticed the carpet was worn and old, but couldn't see the walls very well. His hands were tied in front of him, but not tightly, and when he looked through the eyeholes of what was covering his head, he noticed that his wrists were wrapped together in an intricate design with a black satin ribbon.

A man was on his left side, leading him along gently but firmly; he could tell by the scent as well as a glimpse of dark, muscular legs the color of rich coffee. Walt wasn't scared; in fact, he was trembling with anticipation. The long hallways he walked down were old and faded and dusty, exactly as Jordan had described them. He knew this had to be the place from the dream. Walt was dying to find Jordan there, but believed in his heart that it wasn't up to him.

After walking through a couple of hallways and down two flights of stairs, he was ushered into a room fully decked out in red. He stared in awe and wonder, as best he could, while his hands were carefully untied. The black man turned to Walt, bent down, and kissed him gently on the lips.

"You will find what you came for, my friend," he spoke in a deep voice, "but there may be a cost. To you."

And with that he walked away, leaving Walt standing in the middle of the room, gazing around behind his mask. *So that's what it was*, he realized. Everyone else in the room had one on too. And not much else, from the looks of it.

He looked down and saw he was dressed in nothing but black patent leather shorts, boots that laced up to his knees, and a delicate gold chain connecting his nipples. As he searched for a mirror to check out his mask, he saw it. No, not his reflection.

Him.

Jordan.

He looked magnificent, that much was true—but also quite cruel and frightening. Walt stood still in shock; he couldn't move if he wanted to. His boyfriend was larger than life, that's what it was; he was tall, lithe, oiled up...and evil. He looked like a demon, with glittery yellow eyes shifting behind a hideously gorgeous mask, his tattoos flashing light and color, and a gold outfit that was striking in its construction, fit, and movement, as though it were custom made. The shimmery pouch made his manhood look absolutely exquisite and a supple harness gave him a power that seemed ethereal in some way.

Walt found it impossible to tear his eyes away. And everyone in the room felt the same way, Walt noticed, as he finally shook himself out of his trance. He was mesmerized by just watching Jordan.

The demon was walking as if in slow motion, the air moving thickly around and behind him as he prowled around the room. *He's picking out his prey,* thought Walt with horror. There were three huge men, including Walt's escort, standing guard in the middle of the room watching over Jordan, making sure no one got too close while also allowing Jordan to get to anyone he wanted. The men acted like his security detail, as if they were Secret Service agents or bodyguards. It was fascinating to watch, and at this point, Walt finally felt like he was in a dream.

"This isn't real," he whispered out loud, but no one heard him. Or if they did, he was dutifully ignored.

He swiveled his head behind the heavy mask, noting that the men displayed around the room were unbelievably beautiful, and the few women in attendance were drop-dead gorgeous too. The crowd seemed hand-picked by a movie scout, too perfect to be real, all of them attired in skimpy outfits exuding originality, extravagance, and excessive sexuality. The effect was titillating yet somehow revolting at the same time. So much skin! So much *gold*! Everywhere he looked, red and gold.

Then there were the colors of the masks, the feathers—every possible shade of the imagination. All of the colors made Walt's eyes water. He brushed off the moisture leaking out of his eyes, but his hand's movement seemed to take forever. When he could finally move his legs, he sidled over to the side of the room by the long banquet table, hoping to blend in a bit and see what was up.

While everything appeared immaculate and dignified, he sniffed and smelled something rank. He looked down and saw tiny ants crawling into and over some cheese, as well as a large mound of maggots inhabiting a cantaloupe. He almost gagged with disgust. *Does no one notice?* he thought in wonder. Well, all eyes were on Jordan and on his three "bodyguards," but Walt had a feeling that there was a seedy underbelly here beyond anyone's, especially Jordan's, comprehension.

During Jordan's second loop around the room, he nodded in Walt's direction, barely noticeable, but Walt nodded lightly back. A connection was made.

The room spun in his vision for a moment, flickering like an old movie, and Walt had to grab a nearby table for support. A fly landed on his hand, but he quickly shooed it away and decided to get away from the food. The spoiled rottenness around him was nauseating.

At this point, Jordan was drinking some thick red liquid that looked suspiciously like blood, but Walt didn't know if that was true or if he was letting the surreal nature of the party finally get to him. He did feel dizzy, and Jordan was walking so slowly as to not stumble over himself. What was in that drink?! He saw some of the guys looking pointedly between Jordan and the guards, as if ready to pounce at any moment, and he realized that the hair on the back of his neck was raised in alarm.

He had to get to Jordan. Fast. Or they'd get him. Maybe Jordan wasn't looking for prey. Maybe *he* was the prey.

He saw Jordan nodding to more men while swaying on his feet. Luckily, there was a recliner by his side and he sort of fell down into it, as if sinking under water.

The two older gentlemen closest to Jordan licked their lips and gave each other knowing winks. One of the blond twinks disentangled himself from the other and started making his way over there. Even one of the women, a striking redhead with long hair cascading down her naked back, got up and casually, oh so casually, began snaking her way over to Jordan.

Walt raked his fingers briskly through his beard.

That's it. Gotta move. Now!

He walked over to the divan on rubbery legs and plopped down harder than expected. Jordan stared at him through the tiny eyeholes of the mask, but the yellow orbs registered no flicker of recognition, no welcoming sign whatsoever.

This frightened Walt. He had to get Jordan out of that room immediately, before something bad happened. And something bad *was* going to happen, he could feel it.

That was when Jordan reached over and grabbed Walt's crotch with a sex-crazed look in his discolored eyes. Walt smiled. *Okay, he does recognize me...or at least that one part of me,* he mused. Jordan was undressing Walt with freaky eyes and rubbing Walt's dick until he started to get hard in his little shorts. As his erection grew, men slowly floated toward Jordan from every angle of the room, with the bodyguards allowing full access.

This is it, Walt observed, *whatever it is, it's happening now.* They lurched forward like zombies. As the first person to approach Jordan was reaching out his hand to grab at his little gold cock-sack, Walt panicked and lifted up his mask, startling everyone around him. They scattered like flies. Jordan's yellow eyes opened wide; he looked absolutely petrified, so Walt grabbed his arm and shouted "Jordan!" out loud, suddenly finding himself awake in bed, shaking Jordan's arm and calling out his name.

The timing was odd, because he was doing the same thing at the same time in two different places, but that's how he woke up. And that's how he woke Jordan up.

And that's what he saw in the dream.

Their dream.

Aaron Powell

Aaron Powell is an entertainment industry veteran, having worked in front of the camera and behind the scenes. He started out as a dancer and was able to get work as an extra in old school hip-hop videos and New York City clubs. After a brief stint at Arista he worked at one of the most prominent black-owned PR firms in New York, where the owner took him under his wing and taught him the ins and outs of publicity. Aaron would later branch out and work as a publicist for various radio and TV personalities, and for record labels such as Tommy Boy and Ultra. In recent years he has worked as publicist for TV personality Wendy Williams' last novel *Ritz Harper Goes to Hollywood* and for the late groundbreaking author E. Lynn Harris' final mainstream novel *Mama Dearest*. Aaron lives in New York City.

Can I Have a Taste?

Papi chulo, can I have one taste?
I promise not to waste a drop of your creamy leche.
I think you know I would never hesitate to a playful game of tackle-and-rape with you, a one time dream I wish would soon come true.

You are like my brother from another mother.
We care deeply and look out for each other.
Yet I still need to feel and taste you papi, I want you as my lover.

You have my trust and you know I would never betray you.
I earned the trust you have in me...please amigo let me kneel down to satisfy you.

Just one taste of you is all I want, nothing more would I ask, even though I would always welcome your thick uncut dick deep inside my ass.

You can easily take my culo, and you know I would never bend over to offer it, for fear of losing you.

What will it take?
Will I have to ask you or will you put that pinga in my face trusting I will know what to do?

My fellow Blatino bro you are beautiful inside and out, which makes me want to taste you even more.

Your eyes melt my heart and soul because I know you care, so I would never dare throw myself at you. I just hope when you read this you will make all my wet dreams come true.

Papi, you must know what you do to me, when you smile, look at me and wink. Each time you greet me with a "man" hug, squeezing me so close and tight, I always imagine myself sucking you to sleep each night.

You are so cool and supportive of me being gay and you will always be my homeboy until death takes one of us away.
Until that day, I will wait and I will dream, knowing one day in this lifetime, you'll fill my mouth with your cream.

Brown Sugar Blatino

Every time I see you with your sexy tribal tattoo,
my mind begins to think about deep-throating you.

Your chest is shaved.
Your shoulders broad.
Your open arms are always welcoming and warm.

At the gym you playfully flex for me,
(Which makes me think, maybe you wanna *sex* with me!)
Ay, papi, I wanna feel your brown sugar-dipped dick brush against my
full lips.
I will firmly hold your lean 32-inch waist as you forcefully push that sugar
stick inside my lips.
You force me to swallow deep, making me choke on the width of
that thick cola bottle dick.

My jaws grow weary
My eyes get teary, as I anxiously await the sound of you getting closer to
my soul.
Then I see your head tilt back as your eyes slowly roll.
Come on, papi!
Please splash me with your liquid gold.
Please share with me your juice of life.
The juice which grows your first-born son inside your wife!

Carlos Manuel Rivera

Carlos Manuel Rivera (Carboinael Rixema) is a Puerto Rican actor, poet, and performer, as well as a college professor and researcher. He has performed for more than twenty-seven years in places such as Puerto Rico, Spain, Mexico, and the United States, and has a doctorate degree in Hispanic Theater from Arizona State University (2000). He also published a popular research book, *Popular Theater: The New Poor Theater of America*, written by Pedro Santaliz, as well as a book of poetry entitled *Soplo mágicos disparates* (Orbis Press, 2003). Carlos Manuel is an Associate Professor of Spanish at Bronx Community College, CUNY.

Among his more relevant works are: *The Tempest* by William Shakespeare (actor); *Híbrido* (director); *The Origin of the Sea* by Oscar Giner (actor); *La pastorela* (actor); *Hispanic Zone* with Guillermo Reyes (actor); *La tongo* by Abniel Marat (actor); *Bori-Cuándo* (poet-performer); and *Pastiche* by Roberto Prestigiacomo (performer).

With Pride in the Nationalist Party

A Manuel (Chu) Ramos Otero

Left, Left
Left, right, Left.
Bitch,
sí my Party is Nacional with pride.

If you question
where I'm coming from?
My response is
What you are searching?

Lo que se ve no se pregunta,
valor y sacrificio,
y su encuentro
en amplios radios
de mis trincheras.

With pride
la patria
doesn't deny
to whom is working for it.

The part is for everybody
and of everybody its parts,
From sins until silences.

I'm going to give you lo que me mides.
Y si lo que me mides se convierte
en tus ansias.

Slow down your moving.
Come,

para que la tumba
no se acomode a tus caprichos.

I am here
inventing
that you left
para que no se condicionen
límites ni horizontes en tus medallas.

All of those illusions formed by
your camaradas dejaron
para que me grito
no condene lo que soy,
no cabe dentro de tu Estado.

The Nation is my community,
my imaginaries
the unforgotten root
of your name.

The abject of my shadows,
which pronounces
de tu insensatez dormida
y de tu impúdica magnificiencia,
la codicia
de lo que no se ha fingido.

Here I am
and as a germen
speaking out from virus
the death and the beatitude
be your own Punishment.

Left, Left
Left, right, Left.
¡Viva Puerto Rico libre!

I am Pedro Pietri's Character

Of course, seguro que *yes, to Pedro Pietri*

WARNING:

My citizenship is US, but with an ethnic/racial identity hyphenated by the Hispanic-American-Indian-Post-Asian and Pan-African non-White American. In other words, the Repeating Island: Post-Nuyorican, Post-Puerto Rican-American, Post-Mail (pronunciation in Spanish), Post-Spics, pos, pos, sí how I was telling you…

I am Pedro Pietri's Character,
I am Pedro Pietri's Character.

No
being
allá here.

Anyway
in my way
The Spanish is broken here,
the English is broken there.

Confusion.
Nation.
Action.
Pos, Corruption,
anywhere.

I am Pedro Pietri's Character,
I am Pedro Pietri's Character.

left,
right,
very
ambiguous

Moron,
oxi…
jeno,
oxeno.

I am Pedro Pietri's Character,
I am Pedro Pietri's Character.

From the island,
by the way
de lado
there,
here.

If my island moving there
and it's cool with the mix
I am Pedro Pietri's Character,
I am Pedro Pietri's Character.

De aquí pa'llá,
de allá pa'cá.

Facing here,
broken there.
Floating Island,
fo,
tú apestas.

I am Pedro Pietri's Character,
I am Pedro Pietri's Character.

A Minister
with briefcase,
case,
queso.
Cheese!
photo,
roto.

The Spanish is broken here,
the English is open there.

Dream
America
broken,
token.

No.
oh yes?
MiNation.
The Spanish is broken there,
The English is open here.

-I swear.
-Júralo.
-Lo jugo,
-Hugo.
-Jurakán.
-¡Acángana!
-Dan
ganas de…

The Taínos broken here,
and
the Spanish broken there,
and
The melting don't believe it

I am Pedro Pietri's Character,
I am Pedro Pietri's Character.

(This poem was previously published in the book *Soplo mágicos disparates*, [Orbis Press, 2003])

Sam J. Miller

Sam J. Miller is a writer, a community organizer, and the coeditor of *Horror After 9/11*, a critical anthology forthcoming from the University of Texas Press in the fall of 2011. His work has appeared in literary journals such as the *Minnesota Review, Fiction International, Washington Square, Gargoyle, Fourteen Hills*, and the *Rumpus*. Visit him at samjmiller.com or drop him a line at samjmiller79@yahoo.com

Auschwitz Blowjob

Would I go to Auschwitz? I spent a full week wondering. Walking the street, pacing the supermarket aisles, kneeling in K.'s bathroom in front of him. Would it make me a better person or a worse one? What would it say about me? What kind of person goes to Auschwitz the way others go to Cancún—with a camera and spare cash for souvenirs?

There was no reason to give it so much thought. Going with K. to Krakow was never really an option. He invited me, but he invited a lot of guys. That was the week he was getting tired of me. My time crashing with him was almost up. When K. went to Krakow I'd be back to bouncing from bed to bed to friend's floor to cousin's couch to Port Authority, where I'd have to grub together bus fare and head home a failure, so I had good cause to delude myself to the point of taking Poland seriously.

"Would you want to go," I ask, "to Auschwitz?"

"I don't think I'll have time. You can go, though, during the day while I'm doing radio interviews or other famous global artist stuff."

"But if you had time," I ask, "would you want to go? I mean, does it mean you're a disturbed individual if you go to Auschwitz for a vacation?"

"It'd be intense," he says.

And that's K.: the moody painter looking for good material. Fucked-up relationships; taking in street boys; chatting up the vomit-drenched drunk guy on the subway. K. collects intense experiences like normal people collect CDs. As long as it's intense it's good.

I'm naked at the window from some vague sense that he likes it, that it ties in to his sense of me as a rough little punk, as a hustler, which I'm not, but which I know is important to him. "They say they still have heaps of hair and shoes and eyeglasses," I say.

"That's intense." On his bed, above the covers, he's shirtless, smoking, damp from sweat.

You can't control the heat in his apartment. Either the heat is on or it isn't; when it's on it's way too hot. Huge ancient radiators keep the room parched and uncomfortable from October to April.

"Take those off," I say, turning to him, stroking myself, setting my jaw firm, being butch. The pants come off and he starts on the boxers and I say, "Not those."

Because I know he needs it to get off, I try to be the stern gruff top. I climb up onto the bed and stand on it, in front of him, he leans forward; I push with my hips at the same time as I grab his face and pull it in.

In one of the paintings that got him the invite to Krakow, a boy-packed Abercrombie ad has been chopped up and stuck to the canvas. Blonde boys wearing little on beaches and fields and ski slopes. And then, down the middle, in blood-red drippy paint, are some lines from a poem: every woman adores a fascist/the boot in the face/the brute, brute heart. It doesn't say who said it, and K. didn't get permission from Abercrombie to use their ads, so that painting is probably going to get him sued. But K. would like that.

I yank out, push him back with both hands like I'm casting out a devil. "Stand up," I say, and he does.

"Take off those boxers." He's bigger than me, he's in better shape, he's way cuter. He's independently wealthy. That's why he needs to put himself at the mercy of other men: he's ashamed of his own power. I turn my back to him, put my hands up against the wall, feel the cold cinder blocks under the paint. His building is gross and new, pricey and poorly made.

After sex he says: "I think maybe I will go to Auschwitz, after all. I'll make time for it."

In the morning he's full of ideas, so I have to get out. His apartment is his studio and he can't stand to have people around when he's working. I sit in the park for a while, go the Virgin Megastore on Union

Square and trance out, flipping through CDs without seeing them, thinking. Would I go to Auschwitz?

The only thing that made me consider it, I tell myself, is the hope of getting fucked there. Did the place still have guards? Would they watch you sneak off into the bathroom—or the gas chambers—to get it on? I dream of some brooding Polish peasant, who hangs around the place selling souvenirs, looking for guys like me. There'd be a lot of us. Anybody who goes on a field trip to Auschwitz has got to have conflicting feelings about degradation. As a kid, at synagogue, I knew broads that prioritized Auschwitz just below Jerusalem. What did they get out of that trip? How did it make them feel about themselves, about the world, about being Jewish?

Grey winter clouds wall in Union Square. Cops cuff somebody. Something is dead in the bushes, maybe a man, maybe a squirrel, and its stink gives the cold air a slaughterhouse feel. In spite of everything I don't want to leave New York.

On K's easel when I come in that night is a new canvas, edged in that blood red he's so fond of. Etched in with pencil are two male figures, doing something, I can't tell what. He's testing out a couple different sets of arms on them so they look sort of spiderish.

I never talk about his paintings with him. They make me feel stupid. I never get it, or he makes me feel bad for suggesting there's nothing there to get. That's another reason I'm going to get the boot. But I really don't think there's much to get.

During our after-dinner cigarette he watches his canvas and makes notes in a sketchbook. I watch him. He's really a very gorgeous boy. If he were a little bit more ruthless in bed he'd be perfect for me. When I can tell he's finished I come again to his side, start rubbing his scalp, staring into his eyes trying to get hard. I'd never have stayed so long with someone so unfit for me in bed if I didn't need that bed so badly.

As has been the case for the past three days, it takes me some heavy fantasizing to get through the chore with K. Here's what I'm thinking about:

The day is Poland-late-winter cold. All the way from Krakow, out the windows of the bright shiny modern train, all we've seen are shades of grey. The train chugs me off to Auschwitz: I try to imagine what the trip would have been like by boxcar. Packed with people too poor to have purchased expatriation, too tied to their own grubby hometowns to leave, no matter how bad things got.

The rooms are heated, but not much. Barracks, torture chambers, work halls, mess halls. Dust-free and well lit like art galleries. The smell of piss and terror hangs in the air, faint, like perfume from some woman who walked through five minutes before. Outside, a barbed wire river marks the border between this country and the nation of the living. A tall blond thug Pole named Jarek has come with us from Krakow, sat across the aisle from me, caught my stares and stared back but never smiled. K. figures nowhere in this fantasy. Shutters snap endlessly as our tourist group moves through the rooms, and I position myself again and again by Jarek, behind him, beside him, forcing him to wonder what I want, admiring his ass and the tight fit of his shirt around his shoulder blades— which are strong and sharp, like weapons hidden in his clothes. He slows his pace, falls back; soon we are alone at the rear of the group.

I jam a cigarette in my mouth, tap his threatening back. He turns, cynical grey-blue eyes to make you cream all over yourself, and I make a lighter-lighting gesture with my thumb. "Got a light?" I say in English, but Jarek has nothing but Polish. A handful of ugly words in German and Russian.

His hair is cut Hitler-Youth short, but he's more of a strapping Slav and wouldn't have lasted two minutes under Aryan occupation. He hands me a book of matches and unzips, hauls himself out. An unwashed truncheon. I light my cigarette and he takes hold of my chin, takes away my cigarette with the other hand, puts it in his mouth, pulls me down by the chin. My butt bumps hard against the cinder block wall. From the corner of my eye I see tiny grooves where people clawed at the wall 'til fingernails snapped off.

Some snakes can unhook their jaws to swallow antelopes. I need to learn how to do that. Is there an operation you can get, like getting ribs removed? He gives me a little language lesson, hisses the German words for cocksucker, faggot, subhuman. Halfway through a half hour of steady hip thrusts he pinches shut my nose, which of course I've been relying on for purposes of breathing with my mouth so consummately clogged. Panic flares my eyes and he lets go, and gives me a friendly cheek slap.

When I come the drops glisten on my gut in the gold light coming through K.'s windows—an inheritance, a couple of coins to bribe the ferryman.

J Skye Cabrera

J Skye Cabrera was born in the Bronx, has featured at the Nuyorican Poets Café, Bowery Poetry Club, and City College of New York, and is a member of the New York City Latina Writers Group. She is the speech for those who cannot speak. Her next project is to write a one-woman show; she likes the underground.

Changó Sings to Ochún

I could recall my extra broke phase
Ramen noodles and dollar menu McDonalds® days
And still searching under the crevice of the couch
For small change...
To make my way to the purple haze 7 train
Coming all the way uptown from the BX number 6
I reminisce, as I'd go enamor what
She would call "just a fix"
She lived a few blocks up off of 46th and bliss
This woman was true definition of poetry,
But please allow me to further describe this.
She was Bustelo® dark eyes, brujería in her walk,
And earthquakes would coexist
Within the spiderwebs she spun in the...sway
Of her hips' circumference.
She tastes like the sweetest of all sin
Yet sweet like sonnets off of a 5th page of Anaïs Nin
Body shaped like a baroque violin...
Lips silk breasts, thick like molasses caderas
That birthed melody. Hieroglyphics of love
And tragedy on her skin
Her hair like four winds,
My hands its faithful atlas.
Laying back in "strawberry fields" with a childish grin
Sewing passion within every crevice of her absent aorta's mattress
Yes.
I guess you could say...I was in love.
I was in love.
But we were like Hades and Persephone.
The most obscure of quaint chemistry.
Fire was she. I this caterpillar. She the catalyst exalting

All this creative energy
Like two gods strung out on ecstasy
I still feel her next to me.
Spiritually
Mentally
Especially…
Now that she is gone I am a bachata song on repeat
Drenched in 6 shots of Hennessy®!
In my delusion it appears as if
Romeo seems dirt cheap,
Shakespeare's mere spirit loses sleep,
I am Atlantis steep, Ovid can't even stand next to me
Respectfully.
But I suppose I was the one to double-tie my shoelace and run.
See I am more thorn, less rose.
Much like my father, cock the gun, a coward's sun
Sometime back her mother had passed away,
Swore I would be Spartan-like and stay,
But instead of subsiding
I seemingly amplified her own internal demons
So I left.
And now I part the cages of my teeth to echo this love
You can catch me reckless, every mic across the street,
Hoping it seeps through the concrete
Ricochets to her heartbeat
And transcends like prayer to my gods all up above
My Ochún honeybees weep of offerings so true
I abandoned your body but send my spirits to possess the hands now
possessing you…
I abandoned your body but send my spirits to possess the hands now
possessing you…

Dime sí. Tú piensas volver. Regresamos a lo de ayer. Mujer…tú eres
Amor, guerra y miel.
Dime sí. Tú piensas volver. Regresamos a lo de ayer. Mujer…mi
alma…mi alma se muere.

Pure communism like La Santa María.
I hope my thoughts pierce
Pienso en ella, todos los ocho días...
Y todavía
Her occasional Easter smile.
My god, it's been a while.
But she left fossilized remnants
Running deep in my thoughts like the river Nile
There's still no recovery of my body
I try to reenact. Recall. Orgasmic melodies, interconnect,
Soul-sex, her tongue my favorite hobby.
Go deep. Go deeper, mami. Queen, what I mean is internal,
Is far better 'cause I have loved you since Obatalá
Way back about 3,000 Decembers,
Since our ancestors,
Wore palm trees as skirts and looked up to the blue sky
To predict inclement weather
Since ink first met virgin white
And decided to birth the very first love letter.
Trigger thought. Trigger thought.
Trigger. Let's get together.
'Cause you are not just a house, my dome's home
And so I suppose, you rock the throne
In the architecture of my body,
No other woman is the replacement
If this were a caste system of adoration,
You would be pedestal-high in the attic,
Every other lover, steady low in the basement.
This is nothing basic.
My tongue won't sit complacent.
This is Picasso, Van Gogh, Salvador Dalí conversation
And I know you've got a relation or whatever
But this will serve if ever enemies supersede
And your perception of me they try to sever...
If ever enemies supersede

And your perception of me they try to sever…
But tell your wife I come in peace, to not prepare for war
Verbal swords, words sharp like machetes,
In chivalry I rock the highest score
Changó's daughter—what exactly
Did you think you were in for?

Tod Crouch

Tod Crouch has been published mostly in bankrupted fashion magazines and bear porn periodicals. He has written seven novels, five plays, and three illustrated chapbooks. He's lived in New York for nearly ten years, originally hailing from a small town in Illinois. Tod's most recent fiction can be read at todcrouch.wordpress.com.

The Only Life I Ever Intentionally Ruined

I grew up in a hard-hitting, white-knuckle town, where the boy scouts burned crosses in people's yards for impure blood and got badges for it. My principal was the head of the KKK and the superintendent got caught jerkin' off to 900 phone-sex numbers, but not before expelling a few kids after making them take the fall. We kept our heads down and out of the way, denying ourselves for survival, alone and on the defensive. Even the dudes we slept with at night scorned us during the day. And it kept getting worse. Then one day I went all Michael Douglas in *Falling Down* on their asses and nothing would be the same again.

Some faggot-hating freshman leaned over the seat on the school bus and started digging in with all the god-fearing homophobic hyperactive righteousness of a social climbing wannabe, when I blew the door off the closet: Quarterback Jim was boning Gay Jason. Effeminate Gay Jason arranged meetings with Quarterback Jim from my house, only to be ridiculed by his lover the following day. And The Wrath of Tod would come down upon him. Wildfire took notes on how to spread more quickly from this maelstrom of teenage gossip. In two hours, a posse arrived at my mother's house, ready to beat the shit out of me, though I no longer lived there. I very nearly skipped school the next day, but decided to go in the chagrin of the doomed.

Thrown into high school politics, I denied outing myself—for it would merely discredit me in the eyes of my enemy. Teachers could barely maintain control during class. I fielded the PR catastrophe of outing the golden boy of the football team and Gay Jason, which was no secret to anyone—for Gay Jason boned every dude at that school, except for me of course. As my credibility weathered the storm, my first failed love turned against me, telling everyone I wanted him to pee in my butt. Their counter argument was now, "Hey Tod, can I pee in your butt?" Since Internet porn had yet to prove this possible, I could only one-up them by saying, "I dunno, can I shit in your mouth?"—where they were shocked into silence.

We ate silently while flecks of cooked carrots came our way until Quarterback Jim came at us in a fury of curses. His close friend, camping neighbor, and wrestling partner, Armando, pulled Quarterback Jim aside and told him it wasn't worth it. Armando now fell into suspicion, sending everyone into a Lavender Scare: suddenly everyone was gay, but no one was reaping the benefits. But yeah, Armando was totally tappin' that. We left the outed couple in tears and entered the gymnasium, assaulted by the loudest hate rally ever: pennies chimed off the basketball court, roars of fury deafened louder than any pep rally or homecoming game win. At the other end of the hall, our stout principal waited, arms crossed and scowling because of the mess *we* made, and forbade us from ever coming into the gymnasium again. Fine with me. We ran home that day, the mob following close behind. Luckily, everyone on the track team was gay.

At practice that day, Coach pulled the football team aside at practice and said, "Not anymore. What you are doing is very, very illegal and I can't let this keep happening. If I hear you say anything to those kids, you're not only off the football team, but you're expelled for the rest of the year. I won't tolerate this." Looks like Coach wasn't so bad after all.

Well, Gay Jason ended up on the *Ricki Lake Show*. Armando got married, had two kids, works at a fitness center, and goes camping with his buddies—a lot. Quarterback Jim was the most scorned man in high school, unable to get laid senior year and throughout most of college—nobody loves a gay hypocrite. It just goes to show Quentin Crisp was right: Some roughs are really queer, and some queers are really rough.

Rosalind Lloyd

Bronx-born and bred, Rosalind Christine Lloyd is a contemporary fiction writer, occasional poet, screenwriter, journalist and music reviewer. An acclaimed writer of erotica, her work has appeared in over fifteen anthologies, including *Best American Erotica* and *Best Lesbian Erotica*. She's a graduate of the New School University, with a concentration in creative writing, and also a prodigious blogger. Rosalind lives in Soho with her queer version of a nuclear family.

Deflower

The Union Square Green Market has a certain nuance that cannot be found anywhere else in the city. New Age farmers gather there to hawk agriculturally-sophisticated organic perishables and flora. It was early April and the sun was burning the New York City sky at an unseasonable seventy-five degrees.

A trough of wild orchids: their cups were tiny with colors so vibrant they seemed surreal. After selecting a nice bunch, while waiting patiently to pay, someone's elbow, sharp and swift, violently found its way into my left kidney. Now, I'm what's called a typical New Yorker, in other words, this rude, ill-mannered culprit was about to feel my wrath in the most scathing criticism I could hurl. I looked at the guilty party. Before me was a tight little ass squeezed into a pair of sinfully soft leather jeans. Bent over, this goddess stretched long golden arms sparkling with a thin film of sweat reaching over bouquets of flowers to retrieve her target. Choosing a wild rose a certain shade of pink so luminous it was almost fuschia, she raised the flower to her face, allowing the silky petals to caress her nose. Satisfied, she cupped the bulb within the palm of her left hand, her long dainty fingers tenderly stroking the external smooth petals. I wasn't exactly prepared for what she did next. With her right hand, sinking her long finger into the pistil of the flagrantly pink rose, she penetrated the bulb while her left hand squeezed the silky petals. In a split second, every conceivable part of me capable of becoming aroused was demanding some serious attention.

Severely chiseled cheekbones cradled dark and sultry bedroom eyes that were opened only halfway as if in a perpetual state of arousal. Her short, naturally bushy spirals were streaked in brown and gold hues. Her skin color, glistening in the sunlight, reminded me of Grandma's hot buttered biscuits. Tall and thin, centuries of African royalty seemed embedded in her dignified posture. Full breasts were giving her ultra tight t-shirt a hard time.

Seemingly content with her selection that included the pink rose, she thrust the bunch at the farmer. I couldn't believe her nerve. First, she assaults me; then she molests a defenseless flower; and then she jumped in front of me while in line. Strangely, instead of feeling angry, her aggression turned me on. The farmer handed the roses back to her, wrapped simply in a thin sheet of wrinkled tissue paper tied with sisal. My gullibility expected eye contact with her, when instead, she slammed her entire body against me; breasts, thighs, mounds of Venus all crashing together creating this confused exchange of energy so fast and hard it rattled me, making my head spin. The wind knocked from me, my orchids were tossed to the ground as "leather pants" marched on.

"I think she likes you," the farmer remarked, gathering my orchids and wrapping them for me.

"I don't think so. She practically knocked me over," I answered, attempting to regain my coolness—because my body was vibrating with both pain and pleasure while I watched her escape.

"Well, she asked me to give this to you." In his hand was the fateful molested rose.

Lingering behind her at a safe but interested distance, I watched as she browsed through a few veggie stands before darting across the street and into the Coffee Shop, a trendy restaurant on the square.

Once inside, I didn't see her. Where could she have disappeared to so quickly? With flower in hand, I followed my feminine instincts and went directly to the ladies room.

The door of one stall was open. I could hear a steady tinkle penetrating the ice cold water in the bowl of a toilet. There she stood facing the tank as I peeked in, the toilet seat up, her magnificent naked ass exposed like an epiphany. Her leather pants were down around her knees as she straddled the toilet bowl, peeing standing up as if using a men's urinal. *This* was a woman after my heart.

When she finished, without turning around she said, "Don't just stand there, come in here and lock the door behind you." Her hoarse but terribly sexy voice commanded in a rude whisper.

Standing directly behind this insanely beautiful woman with her pants down around her legs, I slammed the door shut, dropping my shoulder pack and flowers on the floor. Seizing her from behind, I wrapped myself around her like a deprived fiend. One of my hands found and fondled a breast quite warm to the touch. Arousal swept over me like a wildfire threatening to burn me alive, unless I found something wet to put it out with. While brutally swirling a pouty pierced nipple between my fingertips, my other hand went between her legs, dipping caramel fingers in between creamy thighs, sliding inside her hot, slippery wet cunt. My fingers manipulated her inflamed, pulsing clit sheathed in silky moist splendor, causing her to grind her bare ass into my crotch in a very demanding manner.

Balling my hand into a nice grip, I gently buried my knuckles deeper inside her flooding sex, deftly and steadily, stuffing myself so far into her that she whimpered, saturating my hand with soft heat.

Her hands were spread out in front of her against the wall behind the tank—as if under arrest. With her legs spread open over the bowl, I reached for the fateful pink rose. Gliding it across her divine ass, a trail of goose bumps appeared, inciting more of her groans. Tenderly sticking the tip of the long stem of the flower in between her cheeks, I guided the rose downward as if arranging it within the confines of her beautiful, juicy ass now turned exotic vase, thorns pricking her tender skin in its trail. She sucked in bits of air between clenched teeth before moaning sensuously as I continued to slowly slide the flower in between her buttocks, until the bottom of the stem appeared from her ass. Carefully pulling the stem down from underneath her, I made sure the rose was snug tightly in between her ass cheeks. This rocked her, making her quiver and forcing her to whimper a little louder. I grabbed her mouth gently to muffle her. When she succumbed to silence, I licked the back of her neck with cat curls of my tongue. She tasted like salt, body lotion and almond soap, making me wonder what her other wonders tasted like. My licking turned into fevered sucking which caused her entire body to slide around in my arms as if begging me for something. After wiggling the long stem of the rose from between the divide of her ass I lightly brushed its petals along the tiny red imprints left by the thorns, taking broad strokes that gradually developed into a brief round of light spanking. Her sighs provoked me to guide the stem forward in between her thighs, massaging the silky petals against the delicate flesh of her smooth shaven lips. We soon discovered we couldn't exploit the moment any further—as someone entered the bathroom, going into the stall next to ours.

She froze. Gently removing the rose from between her legs, I got myself together, sticking the rose in with my orchids. Repressing the urge to take a playful bite of her ass, I allowed myself one final nibble of her luscious neck before picking up my shoulder bag, unlocking the door and disappearing, leaving her surrendered over the toilet.

In hindsight, I think she learned a valuable lesson about disturbing flowers.

Gabrielle Rivera

Gabrielle Rivera was born and raised in the Bronx, New York. She is a poet, writer, and director. Her first short film *Spanish Girls are Beautiful* explores young Latina queers navigating urban environments and finding love. Her short story "Juliet Takes a Breath" was published in the Lambda Literary Award-winning anthology *Portland Queer: Tales of the Rose City*. Gabrielle is also in the process of writing her first novel based on that short story. She loves craft beer, open mic nights in dirty bars, and zombie flicks.

The Love Choke

Her hands were wrapped around my throat,
using her newly found kung fu grip,
I was slammed against the closet door.
Bewildered, my pulse pounded against the
calloused Newport®-stained fingers that desired to slow its beat.
Sweet—so this is what love is?
Everything froze. We were superimposed
on a black grainy screen,
with the life we shoulda been living
playing on repeat.
Five years have passed between us and it's come down to this
Sink, swim, or die by my hands, bitch.
You coulda been my forever. I never thought it would go down like this.
Fly backwards over hills and pass through the New Jersey Turnpike,
take a left at the Delaware Memorial Bridge and swoop down onto 695 South
and you are in Baltimore, motherfucker...
You were my Starbucks® girl there, the one they all said was *too pretty to be gay* and *you'll never bag that one*, can't you tell the difference between friendly and flirting?
As if I was not even good enough for the coffee girl to wink at...
But you winked and I blinked back and somewhere we found a smile
And then a kiss as you reached out to me and began our bliss,
was this a Frappuccino® Christmas?
I found the kid to my play
The Clair to my Heathcliff.
You rocked my fucking world, baby.
We sang Chaka Khan songs cuz
ain't nobody love me better,
make me happy,
make me feel this way...
It was that type of fucking day.

Looking into your green eyes I saw the mother of a child
that did not exist yet, but now there was a yet,
there was a future bet.
But I forgot that I totally suck at gambling
I never win.
Why try to win back money that was already in my pocket?
Why try to win back a heart I should have never given you in the first
place?
*Note: If a girl gets wasted with you on the first date and does not sleep
with you she's a keeper.*
*Second note: If the same girl gets wasted again on the second date, she
is an* alcoholic.
And you are blinded when you ask for that third date.
Cuz I sealed my own fate and had the audacity to be surprised when I
looked into her blacked-out eyes,
as she had me by the throat five years into that future bet.
At that moment I could taste regret
I could not believe we had let
it get so fucked…
I bucked at the pressure and had to think fast. I outweighed you by at
least 60lbs. I could break at least sixty bones in your face just to get my
heartbeat out of your grasp and yet I let a few more moments pass.
Will I let fingers choking my breath turn me into a wife-beater? Think
about that again. Will I let your violence against me turn into a *tag team*
of my *left* and my *right* breaking your face?
Will that left and that right make this all right?
Make this a pleasant sight?
Will you steal my soul along with my heart tonight?
I will not let you turn me into a wife-beater.
WIFE: *wisdom intoxicating forever epiphany.*
BEATER: *betraying everything after the epiphany is revealed.*
Including myself. I will not be that woman, but I will not die by your
hands.
I used every ounce of restraint and gripped your wrists,
twisting them just so...
Just so I could catch my breath and catch you off-guard enough to get

you to let go.
I pushed you onto the couch and knew it was over.
You woke up the next morning, single and without a single fucking
memory we were superimposed on a black grainy screen,
with the life we shoulda been living
playing on repeat.

Jane Doe Rican

I am the Jane Doe Rican,
another faceless name on the 2010 Census,
like we're senseless,
filling out paperwork for a white man patchwork quilt,
of your household build and makeup,
put your game face on,
get ready for those bright shiny TV lights,
it's conspiracy time for the simple minds,
who put one and one together.
How many documented homosexuals do you have on your block?
Now Uncle Sam's got us on lock cuz we
checked that domestic partner box,
can't just blame the man,
cuz I pierced I's and tatted t's
after updating my various social networking statuses,
pardon my Kanye-ese.
I make syllables work for me.
I am the Jane Doe Rican.
I do as I please.
Got the high-fructose corn syrup OCD,
microwaves and gluten allergies.
All things I dismissed as evidence of
white insanity
have now begun to directly affect me and my native habitat
all my friends' babies are fat
we don't talk, we g-chat, from there we toss back twitter smack,
as if that was as fun as
trading your momma snaps on the playground
those days, our old ways, been long gone and
we don't give a shit—long as we know who Paris Hilton
is trading STDs with
and I don't even know that chick.

Maybe she's a saint
I do know this
The Jane Doe Rican she ain't!
So now you get my odd concerns
Opinions Voiced
Meeting's Adjourned
Nice to meet you,
please forget my face
cuz the Jane Doe Rican
wasn't here in the first place.

Miguel Angeles

Miguel Angel Angeles is a Xican@ migrant born and raised in the Central Valley of California. The youngest child of migrant farm workers, he has enjoyed reading and writing from a young age. He studied Classical Studies at the University of California at Riverside, and having been transplanted in New York since 2005, he is currently completing a Masters in Latin American and Caribbean Studies at New York University. A voracious reader, Miguel has been inspired by the works of Ovid, Catullus, Gloria Anzaldúa, Cherríe Moraga, Arturo Islas, Michael Nava, and Manuel Muñoz to name a few.

Cicatrices

the scars he sees and wonders whether they are really there or not. he remembers the key he used so dull and dirty; pressing hard against his wrist and forearm; the dragging slow and methodically painful; the key too dull to break the skin, the pressing hard enough to break capillaries releasing the sadness within, and yet containing it. it was free from his veins but remained with(in) his body, no longer contained within the miniscule directed paths, free within to wreck havoc upon his every thought, every move, every breath. he remembers then, glancing at the self-inflicted remedy, the burning it brought, the faintest taste of iron as he raised his wrist to his lips, kissing, licking, sucking his wounds. the burning of his mouth on his wounds, his wounds in his mouth. those wounds he sees bright red on almond. he recalls seeing them days later...scars...hopes they will remain there forever and wills it so. he wonders years later whether he wants to see the scars he sees. or needs to. his release valve. his very own personal invisible one-man potlatch.

Mario finds himself licking his lips and looks up. across the great divide he's caught the man's eye and he smiles. eyes darting lazily back and forth, desire entangled. desperate and helpless to tear asunder the ties that bind.

years later that same gaze will serve to reimpose that great barrier that envelops them like some imaginary line in the ground that is meant to separate...will cause them to hide the great love and desire they feel for the other. love for them, after all, had never been innocent, sweet, kindly given. it came with a cost and from children they had paid dearly for the small amounts of affection they had been given or taken.

together they peruse over such feelings, spend Sundays locked in violent embraces, awkward always, but necessary, tears streaming the soaked sheets consuming them. the unraveling always the most difficult for each. the knowledge that they will return to their worlds of solitude, purposely hidden, as they playfully smirk one at the other, driving the daggers back into each other's spine. reopening the wounds they have each nursed to health, that would never close.

he prays daily and visits the river as often as he can. Mario, from a young age, has found the comfort and protection that the river brought. and though he'd been told the horrid tales of La Llorona over and over as a child, to beware her (intending to instill a fear in him that was never meant to last), that she would take him too in her efforts to (re)cover/(re)place her lost children, he feared not this weeping wailer of a woman, for he knew that unlike the others he was a legitimate child, the one she sought after so often to love and protect. El Llorón. those nights his father would come home drunk, she proved that. when everyone became entangled in the brawls so he couldn't tell whose limbs struck whom, he would run and hide in the closet and feel her embrace so that he was able to emerge.

now, as he prays to La Llorona Yoruba; he thanks Iyalorde for her touch, for Tocallo, and the pain that brings such life. Mario knows his beloved 'Callo was a gift from Iyalorde; that night on the train he found himself craving more wounds. that gaze…that bellicose gaze that would bring pain and rebirth…

and so he prays…

maferefun Oxum[1]
gran reina de las aguas
frescas y dulces[2]
i come to you, 'Ama[3]

---

[1] Praise to Ochun

[2] Great queen of waters fresh and sweet

[3] mom

and bring you this
humble libation
de lagrimas y miel[4]
s a l e n d u l z a d a[5]
gran virgen de
la caridad[6]
bring me all for
my survival
sadness and joy
dolor y amor[7]
death and rebirth
desesperación y esperanza[8]

the horrifying love they gave to one another so frequently; the shouting from a pain more meta than physical. catching the other's thrust, the one would return it as fiercely; their loving a battle that neither wanted to win nor lose.

when they were done they would lay deep in waiting. hours silent. holding each other captive, the battle ever raging on. typically it would be Mario that would surrender.

"Espe', tell me something," Mario requested, desperate to break the silence and the spell it brought.

"i'm hungry, son. go make me a sandwich. it's the least you can do."

"fuck you 'Callo, i ain't your bitch, go make it yourself. And don't 'son' me. You ain't my daddy," Mario, snapped in frustration.

---

[4] Of tears and honey

[5] Salty-sweet

[6] Great virgin of charity

[7] Pain and love

[8] Desperation and hope

"That's not what you were shouting an hour ago," quipped 'Callo, his winking accentuating the wicked smirk ever-present on his face.

"Shut up, 'Callo." It took all he had within him to control his laughter, to keep it hidden and hold his stern face of anger.

"¡Dámelo, papi, dámelo! ¡Soy tu perra, papi![9]" He said it so enthusiastically, so seriously, that both couldn't help but burst into a fit of laughter.

Mario slugged him on the arm. "I do not sound like that, cabrón!"

and so it so often goes. Existo, ya no me ignoras[10]. the silence never fails to remind him of the existence which has become his rebellion, his own battle against others' discomfort with ambiguity.

he has no problem naming himself loca[11], puto[12], maricón[13], or mayate[14]. rather than reject those terms meant to hurt and dissuade him from the true path determined for him, meant to instill an inferiority that his persecutors themselves feel, he embraces them and makes them his own. those terms. it's my rebellion that scares them so, he thinks. his rebellion that makes him love 'Callo as much as he does, his rebellion that has made him surrender himself to him completely and make himself his since that night they first met and became intertwined in this maddening, blinding, deafening love that is all their own.

---

[9] Give it to me, daddy, give it to me! I'm your bitch, daddy!

[10] I exist, don't ignore me anymore.

[11] crazy (woman)

[12] bitch

[13] fag

[14] fag (but also used as a derogatory term for African-Americans amongst by some Xican@s)

Orlando Ferrand

Orlando Ferrand is a Cuban-born poet, writer, and interdisciplinary artist. He studied English Language and Literature, Creative Writing, and Comparative Literature at Columbia University and CUNY. His first book of poetry, *Citywalker,* was published in 2010. He's been featured in various anthologies of poetry and essays in the US and lives in New York City.

Signs of the Beloved

for my life partner Joey Medina

They had promised me footpaths
And tropical pathways
They had promised me mirages that I never saw before

That never touched my feet
Until you came

Baptized in the river
by John
And your blue smile
And your eyes of pure honey
Navigating my entrails

I want to be his sea
And his horizon
The rope that rescues his shipwreck

And the word Love
shattering my veins

I am the friend
Sowing sunflowers
To adorn all your corners

When you return
To my woodcutter arms
To my feet
Skilled in the art of mapping uncertain territories

Let's take a walk

When the evenings
Light the sky with rosy-orange-purple swirls

Listen to my voice
When I whisper magic words
To entice the charm of life

Come and let's dive into the mystery
Now when the sea sustains us
Like gods fallen asleep
Who wake up and recover their memories.

New York, 2010

Down-Low

Mother Nature cleanse me please,
I've been banging my head against your walls
uttering the silent words that He can only hear

This is the first rain we've had since the oil spill ceased
in the Gulf of Mexico
and this is the first time I've seen you in months

I asked to not text message my phone;
it destroys language,
my ability to communicate complete feelings in complete, desperate
demands

Jose, the teacher who hangs out in the park with the teens
he does them all at once
the man who doesn't know who he is

The man who still lives with his mother and wife and kids
and always lies about his whereabouts
Mother Nature

I have faith that the fuel running through my veins
is going to be transformed in rain, pure rain
like the one You are sending to the shattering skies

To cleanse my body
and my tongue
needless to say the smashed corner of my down-low heart

And the other one is also Jose
Dominican Jose with wife and kids
who likes a real man, like me, to love him as a God

Mother Nature cleanse me, please
perhaps I am the one who is killing love
before its arrival

I don't bring them over,
I do not desire any of these Joses to visit my temple
or to text me 'cause it kills my capacity to tick Your words

None of these Joses is going to be loved by me
the way I love Mother Nature,
I won't drop a tear over these brown leaves on the ground

for Joses, who pretend they don't know me
when
I show up at the pickup spot on the down-low

to be rained on
by Mother Nature
cleansing itself

Warmhearted tending to my needs
to be embraced
and flushed again back to life

As she does with pollution,
with what does not belong to the flow of love
regardless

There was an oil spill in the Gulf of Mexico
for more than three months
and the human gesture of these men on the down-low

missing in action
recklessly poisoning the gentleness
that grows in every encounter with Mother Nature

Cleanse Me, Please.

New York, 2010

The Fool on Bronx Park East

for Charlie Vázquez

Of Rosewood, the handle of his umbrella
I see him every day from Dusk to Dawn
flailing his skeleton umbrella under the sun
and the moon and the Milky Way
over the cars on the highway
almost naked
the bum
the man who never sleeps
unless
it's raining

He lives under its sheltering frame
He has already surrendered to the hunk of the cars
they stop to let him walk in his ragged underwear
giving them weather advice
drunk driving advice
parental advice, and marriage counseling advice
the bum
the man who never sleeps
unless
it's raining

His umbrella is the remainder of a parachute
perhaps, left by an angel in his ascension to the skies
And the fool on Bronx Park East
aids the drivers bumper to bumper
opening and closing his skeleton umbrella
up and down the highways
the bum

the man who never sleeps
unless
it's raining

The umbrella and the umbrella man
have both lost their skin down to the bones
I am convinced he is the angel
who's lost his wings
and got stuck in New York
without a map of the heavenly skies
the bum
the man who never sleeps
unless
it's raining

The skeleton has resisted the corrosive action
of the elements
the umbrella man is attached to his umbrella
as an umbilical cord
limbically connected
to his bygone memory
the bum
the man who never sleeps
unless
it's raining

I ask myself: is there a need for skin
when you wear your soul inside out
protected
by the celestial
skeleton
of an umbrella?
the bum
the man who never sleeps
unless
it's raining

The Fool on Bronx Park East
run over by the siren
of a chasing highway patrol car
lets me handle and inspect his umbrella
while they dial 911
to safe his skeleton
the bum
the man who never sleeps
unless
it's raining

Make sure she's alright, buddy!
he whispers
the highway is uncomfortably silent for a minute
a thousand headlights flashing
in the middle of the night
and then it rains, just for him
the bum
the man who never sleeps
unless
it's raining

And I examine his umbrella
to make sure it's not been hurt
at his request
I examine his skeleton umbrella
the angel's parachute
that let him land
so low
so far from God
So close to the irony of life
the fool is gone

And I am left alone
with The Nose Cap, The Collar, The Tip-Cup

The Hand Spring, the Tube, The Runner,
The Inside Rosette, The Stopper Pin, The Stretcher,
The Tip, The Rib, The Tie,
The Prevent, The Inside Cap, The Notch
The Outside Rosette, The Open Cap
The Fit-Up, The Ferrule, The Rosewood handle
The umbrella, parachute to help me land
has grown its skin again; it's not a fragile frame.

New York, 2010

Nyna

Nyna is an author, filmmaker, spoken-word performer, and musician. She is infamous for her spoken-word performances in New York's women's scene, as well as in the women's communities of Berlin and Vienna. Her films have been selected for screenings at the *Berlin International Film Festival, New York's NewFest, OutFest of Los Angeles*, as well as international film festivals in Frankfurt, Jerusalem, London, Munich, Oslo, Philadelphia, and Sydney, Australia. A new film based on her novel entitled *"A Kiss from Africa"* will begin production in 2011. She holds a master's degree from the Juilliard School in New York.

Short Story: A Fish Tale

Inspired by a boat trip from Ambergris Caye to Belize City.

She begged to go scuba-diving and wanted me to come along as her swimming partner. They told us to wear a t-shirt to keep the oxygen tank from resting directly on our skin, and to provide some cushion against the straps. I didn't want to worry about my contacts getting fucked up at fifty feet below sea level and needing to squeeze my fingers beneath my mask to try to put them back in place. So I left my contacts at home. I would wear my glasses until we jumped off the boat. I knew I wouldn't be able to see as well. But hey. Seeing the brightly neon-colored fish, and flashy coral reefs with swaying ocean plants, all slightly out-of-focus, would be an experience in itself.

It was a warm, partly cloudy day. Beams of light filtered through the waters, disbursing reflections through the depths. Schools of fish caught my eye as flashes of light, flakes of reflected sun. The sound of my steady breathing, the intake of air from the tube to my oxygen tank, the exhaling of bubbles rising to the surface. This steady rhythm guided the speed of my kick. *Breathe in: Kick 1, 2, 3, 4. Breathe out: 1, 2, 3, 4.* Gone were all earthly handicaps. I was weightless, a gliding entity, moving, seeing, breathing underwater.

There was my Honey. She swam alongside me to see if I was all right. She knew I left my contacts at home and that I couldn't see too far. We conversed via rehearsed hand signals, giving each other the "okay" sign. She glided along in front of me; her long legs kicking in streamline motion, the outline of her muscular ass fading off in the distance. I saw the purple strip on her black bathing suit. She stopped to observe a school of small bright green and neon-blue fish. They peered right into her mask, curious to see who she was. I felt a slight brush on the back of my leg. A baby stingray had come to play with me. Her long, wavy strokes made her look like she was flying. She circled around and came back to swim right over my head. She went beneath my body, ten to twenty feet below, disappearing into the depths. Then I saw the black upper side of her body zigzagging up toward me again. Her eyes came close to my mask. She looked right at me and turned her body upward to reveal her soft, white underbelly. I felt a slight current, as she flapped her fins and deftly changed direction at the last split second, just barely missing my face. She must've known from my unfocused eyes that she had to get close to me for me to feel her, to feel that she was friendly and wanting to play.

I felt another brush on my legs. But this time the fish was much faster. A flash of silver disappeared in the shadows. I saw other flashes of similar colors, rainbow reflections distorted and fuzzy, but identifiable as the same species of fish. I turned to follow them. They swam deeper toward the ocean floor. Reefs gave way to rocks, then large stones and formations. There were patches where the light of the sun could not reach. There were caves down there! That's where the bright, large, sparkling creature had disappeared. I looked for my colleagues. They were nearby. If anything happened, I could've easily gotten to them in time. I entered the cave's mouth.

By the time my eyes adjusted to the darkness, I was aware that my breath-rate had increased; the slight anxiety from the darkness, from no longer being able to take advantage of the sun's reflections; my only visual aid had been taken away. I could only look with my back to the opening, to search for something that might catch a glimmer of light. A cloud must've been overhead. The little bit of sun had dimmed.

What was that?! Something passed in front of me. I couldn't see what it was. It was too dark to see anything. *That's something else!* It slid right across my ass. I felt the soft scales of a very large fish. But wait. Something was under me. Something was touching my stomach. But it wasn't a fish. Those were hands. Human hands. Soft feminine hands.

Had another scuba diver followed me into this cave? I felt the unmistakable tickle of human hair, the hair from the top of someone's head. I reached down and felt a face, but there was no mask, and no tank. All I felt was smooth unencumbered flesh. She pressed her face into my belly, gently easing herself under my floating t-shirt. Her soft lips and tongue made a trail along my skin. *It must be my Honey. She followed me here.* I focused on my breath-rate to keep it calm and steady.

Human arms encircled my thighs. Hands grabbed my ass and searched for the elastic of my swimsuit bottom. I felt a naked female breast pressing against my legs and thighs, while a face burrowed itself into the triangle where my thighs met. *Inhale: 2, 3, 4. Exhale: 2, 3, 4.* The trail of bubbles showed me which way was up toward the surface. The hands succeeded in pulling my swimsuit bottom down to my knees, and further down to my ankles. I had to pull a foot out of them to maintain my kick. I turned my body around to look toward my seducer; her nuzzling in my crotch more urgent, more precise. Free of my swimsuit bottom, I floated with my legs spread wide apart, the open mouth over my clit, the slippery, slick, hot tongue sliding over my succulent, throbbing lips. *But what is this?* Another current of water and another pair of arms encircled my shoulders; fingers caressed the back of my head. Delicate feminine hands touched my face. Deft agile fingers unfastened and removed my mask, the water flooded my eyes—I could never keep my eyes open underwater. Now I had to keep them closed until I found my mask. *Maybe if I swim straight down...perhaps it landed on the ocean floor.*

But the arms around my hips held me fast. And the new pair of arms guided my head against a soft human belly. They swam so effortlessly, whoever those women were. I couldn't see a thing. But my skin was alive with the electric sensations from their touch. The woman above me ran my face along her body. She must've been perpendicular to me, as I felt a wave of current from left to right. The face between my thighs was licking furiously. My climax was imminent. I felt the shift along my face— first belly, then chest-bone, then a soft bosom was caressing my eyes, her nipples hardened in response to the friction. My breath was quickening. I was hyperventilating concentrated oxygen. I knew I was about to come. I took one more deep breath, then removed my mouthpiece and clutched onto it with my fingers, my literal lifeline. At least we were in warm Caribbean waters. My body arched. I was suspended, floating in the primordial womb. I convulsed in spasms of liquid pleasure. I exhaled through my mouth and released a low, gurgling moan, a column of bubbles rose to the top of the cave. The woman above me took advantage of my mouth being free and open and guided her erect nipple straight into it. Still holding my breath, I licked and lapped at it hungrily. Hands stroked and caressed me, arms held me tight. I needed another breath. I gently pulled my lips free and put my mouthpiece securely between my teeth. *Inhale slowly: 2, 3, 4. Exhale slowly: 2, 3, 4.* Gradually my breathing went back to normal. *But what's this?* The breasts on my eyes were moving quickly to my right and I felt the distinct flip of a fishtail: a long, large, elaborate tail. I still felt hands and arms along my body, but there were also the unmistakable cool scales of a fish's skin. No. Two fish. Or was it three? I was too disoriented. *What's this? Oh. I must be on the sea bottom and I just happened to place my hand directly onto my mask. Or...is it being handed to me? Are those fingers? A hand giving my mask back to me?* I pulled it over my head. They taught us how to empty the water out by tilting the head back and exhaling through the nose. Yes! It worked. Now I could open my eyes again. *Ah. There's the cave opening.* All I had to do was follow the light. But I didn't see anyone else. They must've already gone ahead.

I emerged from the cave and found my colleagues all circled around the instructor, his bright reflector strips clearly visible from a distance. They pointed toward me and motioned for me to join them. They weren't so far away. Thank goodness my t-shirt was long enough to hide the fact that I was bare-assed underneath. My Honey was the first to come to me. She asked via hand-signals if I was okay, and I nodded that I was. The instructor gave the thumb-up sign and we inhaled and slowly rose to the surface, exhaling all the way. I was surprised that I didn't need more oxygen, the distance seemed so far.

We finally reached the surface. My lover took her mask off. "Where were you?" she cried. "We thought you were lost."

"I thought you were in the cave with me," I said.

"What cave?"

Uh-oh. How was I going to explain this one? And who? I mean, what...?

"Let's get back in the boat," I said.

I waited until everyone else climbed up the steps so that no one would see my naked butt. Safely back in the boat with all our fins tossed in a heap at the back, I immediately tied a towel around my waist. The swimmers chatted excitedly about the various kinds of fish they had seen.

"Anybody see any mermaids?" the instructor asked jokingly.

All the others laughed. I smiled to myself, staring into the water the whole trip back, wondering if my seducers were following us under the boat.

Karen Jaime

A New York-based spoken word/performance artist, cultural activist and writer, Karen Jaime served as the host/curator for the Friday Night Slam at the Nuyorican Poets Café from 2002-2005. A graduate of Cornell University, Jaime has performed at The Public Theater, The Town Hall, Dixon Place Experimental Theater, the Bronx Academy of Arts and Dance, the Nuyorican Poets Café, Bowery Poetry Club and other performance venues alongside numerous colleges/universities throughout the Northeast and Latin America. Jaime was recently featured in the Emmy-award winning CUNY-TV show "Nueva York" and has appeared in spoken word documentaries such as *Spit!* alongside Nuyorican Poets Café founder Miguel Algarín. A doctoral candidate in the Department of Performance Studies at New York University, Jaime received a 2003 Rockefeller Humanities Research Fellowship, and is currently completing work on a dissertation that focuses on spoken word, slam poetry, and hip-hop theater.

Smells Like Home

I walk in
And *THAT* smell
fills my nostrils to the brim.
THAT smell.
That warm,
gooey smell
of Dominican cakes sold by the slice
and dulce de coco squares
over dulce de leche squares
on cake pedestal stands
with aguacates
underneath—
and the single serving
Chiclets® boxes
coming in flavors like
yerba buena
aka
spearmint
mixing in with the
clear plastic wrapped
caramelo cubes
that decorate the counter,
and the bread case…
Full of pan de agua to your right,
while the guayaba squares are to your left
and there is the radio with the bachata playing
and the smell…
THAT smell…

Of plátanos
And frutas tropicales
in wooden crates

and the narrow
aisles full of Mistolín®
on one side
and the velas—
all the prayer candles—
Santa Bárbara,
I mean Changó,
would be proud
on the other.
And there Is that smell
Of Old Spice®
worn by men
like my grandfather
sporting guayaberas,
mixing in with the smell of
Country Club® sodas.
Looking like Rainbow Skittles®:
Yellow for merengue
Red for fresa
Orange for naranja
And purple for uva,
next to the forest green
Presidentes®.
All cold
and frothy,
front and center when you open the cooler door
Y ese olor
a cerveza
y a comida
that someone brought him
during his lunch hour
from the Dominican joint
around the corner.
That smell of aluminum tins
full of maduros
and arroz y habichuelas

and there is that smell
of calixos—Dominican flip-flops,
slapping on sidewalks
as we chase each other,
my cousins and I,
poking each other
with the needles from the lime tree out front.

It's *THAT* smell—
of loud ass kids
with that in-between hair
cause they're jabao,
high-yellow/red-bone,
of ladies just in from the salon—
there is nothing
like hair that is blown out by a Dominican
seriously—
looking to cool down with a cold one
'cause you know they don't want to sweat it out
and that smell of Santo Domingo
carried in carteras de pana
y zapaticos de charrol
and cousins
and aunts
and uncles
and that smell
that smells *nothing* like
what's outside the doorway—
this bodeguita *doesn't* smell like
the liquor that is poured on the sidewalk
for those that aren't here anymore.

It *doesn't* smell like the fumes
from the markers that have been used
to tag the wall next to the pictures placed above:
RIP: (insert non-government name here).

For those who have been baptized by the street
rituals and burials
don't involve caskets
street cred is solidified
through makeshift altars
that celebrate a life
ended too soon,
while tags commemorate
how the badge of honor was earned...

And there is that smell,
THAT smell
seeping out the door of the bodeguita
as if to say
This wouldn't have happened there,
at least not in this way...

THAT smell
mixing in with the cigarettes
of the women hanging out their windows
shadowed by curtains that always bear fruit
THAT smell
of Agua Florida®
And Johnson and Johnson Baby Powder®
of La Duana
of Bay Shore
of Brentwood
of Washington heights
of Lawrence, Mass.
of pesos dominicanos
taped behind store counters
next to the cash registers
and that damn smell
that washes over me
and wraps me up in a hug
and I am warmed by nostalgia,

reminding me that
this bodeguita
tucked away
around the corner
that I rarely go into
reminds me of something
not very common
but all too familiar
and I realize that
this place,
this space

smells like home...

Roy Pérez

Roy Pérez is Cuban-American, born in Los Angeles and raised in Miami. He is a founding member of the Birdsong Collective and Micropress in Brooklyn, New York. He has three projects underway, including *Inch Back: Love Poems*, a novel tentatively titled *Clouds, Birds, Jet*, and his doctoral dissertation on queer figures in Latin@ literature, performance, and popular culture. He currently teaches Latin@ cultural studies at Wesleyan University. He would like to thank Tommy Pico for the reason, Matthew Pardon for the faith, and so many lovers, most recently, for the substance.

Lucha de gigantes (19° 25' 33" N, -99° 11' 09" W)

I. North

Autodiálogo en el museo embrujado, in
situ
y concreto: this is our colonial
encounter.
A decimation of wax droids under miles
of thick hemp weaves, a mess of
machines
and mistakes. I imagine
your lover Rubén trapped
in a diorama on the theme of industrial
nepotism, the absence of choice, his
mannequin
in a shirt and tie, in rubber and black
wool. The workmen in the family
warehouse follow his soft bark, his soft
bark, his bark. Éste es:

EL NEPOTISMO TRÁGICO.
FRESA URBANA TÍPICA EN SU SITIO
DE EMPLEO
año 2007.
CERA, LANA, SUDOR y PLÁSTICO.

II. South

I've seen so little of your face.
I've seen so much of your hair.
We're taught that we share nothing but
sacrifice, sun worship, plunder,

and priapic gods.
We orbit each
other through
    corridor,
    corridor,
    corridor,
and when we run out of history we sit
on a concrete block, on a concrete
lawn and withdraw.
You wax on Rubén.
I wax on you and I think,
    We are giants to have commanded so
                much.
      We must be giants to have roped
          ourselves down so.
            -Son gigantes.
               -¡Y viven?
            -Casi. Caminan
      con paso de metabolismo flojo.
    -Tienen sed de monstruos lánguidos,
                 semi-
        enfermos, acosados
    y con todo y eso, ¡vuelan!

III. East

The Olmec flyers climb to the top of a
wooden
pillar and leap, suspended by their
ankles, by ribbon,
by nothing.
You let them mesmerize you.
I let you mesmerize me and I
think, we are not ancient
anymore, but I do wish

we could fly, each a sarcophagus,
bound.
It is inhuman,
      it is inhuman,
            it is inhuman every
pose and superstition, every straw-filled
          monument, our colonized bodies
                    seeking rule.
      -Los voladores de Papantla no caen.
                     Nosotros si
            caemos, ellos no caen.
                        Caemos.

IV. West

I begin an ekphrasis of us sitting here:
Clay, saline, glass,
cotton, nylon, animal hair.
Loathsome, fabulate nomads shrouded
in nuclear debris and suspended a fixed
distance
by a thread in a shoebox.
Red giants lumbering inelegantly
through
the museum, its gardens, its superfluous
shop
in which I buy a postcard I will mail to
you
a year from now so that I can tell you,
           We are forensic wonders,
              we were so big! Too big
      to belong to each other we belonged
              to this place instead.

The First Night is the Safest

I wake from a dream shocked to have dreamed
     about you, dreamed we moved far too fast, risked
          far too much for waking life, and to the back

of your neck I say that tonight it's enough
     to have guided the pincers of my thrall
          through your grooves, among your fleshy

effects, into your genes, to have had your
     halves cleft against my hips, to have rent
          you wide on your hinges, along your spine,

to have read your wet back bones touch by
     touch as you straddled my length in the
          blue, and I say that if you were to wake

now, to wake now and reach for me, even
     just barely reach, enough to let me know that
          I can, I will inch you back into night and out

          of sleep, ease you open once more before
     dawn, before time picks
up again, before we
realize the
cost.

Once a Year We Spoon and Edge Under Rules Too Strict and Too Hard But I Heed

Sweat strung and pooling moan for moan I heed, this time while I collect your funk with my hand as a sign of my progress and you get it, you bring it to your mouth and nose and inhale me smelling like you smelling your hair, while you with the small of your back and your tailbone search where you always do for my love and find it wrapped around my thighs, buried behind my stomach, set for you to direct its speed and I heed, moan for moan I heed, because despite this mad infrequency you and I and this are like nothing else.

Alicia Anabel Santos

Alicia Anabel Santos is a proud New York-born dominicana, self-identified Latina lesbian writer, performance artist, producer, playwright, and activist, who decided to write her own tales that honor women throughout Latin America, while also being representative of the American-born Latina experience. She attended New York University and Rhode Island College, is completing a historical novel titled *The Daughters of the Revolution,* and is workshopping her one-woman show *I WAS BORN.*

Alicia is the founder and CEO of the New York City Latina Writers Group, of which there are now over 180 members. An article she published in *Urban Latino Magazine,* "Two Cultures Marching to One Drum," gained the attention of producer Renzo Devia, and their collaboration will change the way the world sees color and race relations in Latin America. In 2008, Alicia joined Creador Pictures as writer and co-producer of its first documentary, "Afro Latinos: La historia que nunca nos contaron." She lives in Harlem with her eighteen-year-old daughter Courtniana. Info: http://findingyourforce.blogspot.com/

I Was Born ~ (an excerpt)

VERONICA (sitting)

Mari, me tenía loca…she drove me crazy and I haven't even kissed her yet. She came into town to see me…it was the first time we were going to be intimate…the moment I saw her walk into the room I felt her electricity. That moment was magic!

That first time was a spiritual experience.
She said our first time
felt like her first time…
que se sentía como un amor virgen…a virgin love…

When love begins…it's beautiful
When love begins…it's light
When love begins…it's a fairytale
When love begins…past loves no longer exist
But virgin love…
Ah, virgin love…
This love is…
Pure love
Innocent love
Unquestioning love
Trusting love
True love
Real love
Full of passion kind of love
Not caught up in the bullshit love
Lasting love
It's you and me love…
Untainted love
Loving you freely *love*

Without conditions love
I feel you inside of me…te siento por dentro de mí…in a way I have
never felt anyone love
You the mirror image of me love ~

Ese momento…when one gives themselves over – que uno se entrega ~
and becomes one ~ now that is love ~

That moment…ese momento…when we gave our bodies to each
other…
felt like the first time…
it was our first time ~
first time we trusted…
we chose each other…
we surrendered completely…to one another…
un amor puro…
This pure love…
This natural love…
This innocent love…
Al principio…we were scared to touch each other…neither one of us
wanted to make the first move…cautious…because this moment was
sacred…there was a moment we questioned…but we released all of
that.

When we first touched…cuando ella me tocó…the moment we locked
eyes…ese primer beso…that first kiss…when we held hands…her
touch…the connection was incredibly intense and immediate. When we
made love…our union…bodies connecting…breasts touching…her
scent…her skin…her neck, our legs intertwined, our sweat…our hearts
beating at the same time…the earth underneath shifted just a little bit. It
shifted into place…all was right…perfection…this was right ~ she said
she was complete ~ we both knew that this was real ~

¿Quién eres tú?

Who am I?

Soy tu madre – I am the woman who gave birth to you…I am where you get your strength…who worries about you even though you're a grown woman…I'm proud of who you are, who you're becoming…the world is a better place because you were born…
I watch over you…
I protect you…
I love you more than life…
Soy tu tía…I am your aunt and godmother…la mujer que te ama tal como eres…happy when I know you're coming for a visit…it's those little things that mean so much…
Soy tu abuela…madre de tu madre…as your grandmother I've raised You as if you were my own…you are a part of me…
Soy tu hermana…I am your sister…proud of all you've accomplished. I look up to you for guidance…turning to you for advice…

Who am I?
I am the woman who cleans your streets and gets paid scraps…
I am a photographer and a producer
I am a businesswoman
I work hard to provide for our family
Every day I'm hustling…
I cook, I clean, I raise our children
I am a hairstylist
I teach you about the importance of preserving our culture and our language…to not sell out for the U.S. visa…

Who am I?
I am the purest form of love…I am the innocent…the untouched…untainted by life's cruel people…

I am that little girl dancing for fun...but also because I am being exploited...and if you like how I dance and give me money...I can put food on the table...
I am the girl who dreams of being a basketball star
I am the girl who believes that when I grow up...I will be...a doctor and veterinarian...so I can return to my barrio and share all I've learned...

Who am I?
I am the girl...with the smile that lights up a room...
I am going to Brown University, Columbia, Yale, or maybe Berkeley ~ my opportunities are limitless...I believe in me and know that I can have all I desire...and ever dreamed of...I am the girl who wants someone to believe in me...someone to rescue me...I'm waiting for that man with the blue passport to whisk me away with him...I am that girl who wonders...*Why did my own mom drop me off at the strip joint to work?...*I am only 16!
I have faith
I want to hold on to hope
A part of me wants to believe and see something more...but my reality shows me a different truth...
I am the little girl whose childhood is being stolen from her...

Who am I?
I'm not concerned...in the meantime I will put on my heels and play...I will play all day...
I am free...I am happy...
I am the future...
I am your best friend...who always walks with you.
I am your inner circle...your support system...I'm in your front row...
I am your safe place to turn to...I bring you peace and love...

Who am I?
I am your rock...your ace...I got your back...I'll bring the Vaseline®...you bring the rings...

Who am I?
I am the Mexican anthropologist studying and investigating the Latino…
I am the historian writing women into the textbooks…fighting for
Women's and children's rights in Peru ~
I am the Hip Hop artist…straight out of Honduras…breathing life into the
world…
I am a writer…my tears on the page…showing the world that tears are a
form of strength not weakness…tears cleanse…helping to purge all the
BULLshhhhhhhhhh you would have me believe to be the truth…put that
in your pocket…hold that ~
I am a storyteller…my stories are the keys that unlock the doors to your
future…¿Si no sabes de donde vienes, cómo vas a
saber para donde vas?…if you don't know where you come
from…how will you know where you're headed…?

Who am I?
I am wisdom…Mother Earth…the reason you were born…you owe me
something…you have a responsibility…turn to me for the truth…
write our stories…

Who am I?
I am a force kid…the force…
I am a producer and writer…traveling the world…learning about Who we
really are….
I am a mother
I am a lesbian
I am all that is right in the world…

Who am I?
I am a woman who knows I never walk alone…
Who are we?
We are the powerful Latina WOMYN changing how society views
us…we are gay, bi, trans, straight, feminist, activist, educators,
filmmakers, policymakers, singers, dancers, athletes, artists, mentors,

visionaries, dreamers, lovers…with pelo bueno, pelo malo, no pelo…black, white…we fight for human rights.
We are the ones writing our stories…who are we…we are the women you never see coming!

Who am I?:
¿Quién soy yo?

I am everything these women are and more…each woman I've met has left her mark on my soul…

Who are we?

We are the WOMYN writing HER-STORY…
so we are NO LONGER LEFT OUT OF HIS-STORY…
I know who I AM – ¿QUIÉN ERES TÚ?

PEACE ~

Tomas Rafael Montalvo

Tomas Rafael Montalvo is an Afro-Cuban Boricua poet who was born in Bayamón, Puerto Rico, and was raised in the South Bronx and Queens, New York. Becoming a poet/spoken word artist came to be after being homeless at one point in his life, being an addict, growing up bisexual in a homophobic household, and having to experience abuse from loved ones; it was not until he started reading in public that he came out about his sexuality. He would like to travel to amazing places, to continue meeting wonderful people, and to have his dreams come true.

The Man I Need

I love when you stand behind me
wrapping your arms around me ever so gently.
In a rough, yet warm, embrace slowly turning me around
placing your hands on my face.
Your fingers running down my chest
making a quick pause at my nipples.
Continuing down my abdomen
until you reach my waist.
Squeezing right above my pelvic bone
I let out a moan...UMMM!
This will be my hands' resting place.

I will gracefully accept all sensitivity you bring out in me.
Like when you bend me over the couch
One hand around my neck, the other covering my mouth
Whispering in my ear, "You are my bitch."
Whispering in my ear, "Say my name, daddy."
Say my name as you penetrate me
with such delicate roughness, full of passion.

In and out I start to moan
gripping the pillows tighter and tighter
telling you, "faster, harder."
Harder and faster as you hit places in me,
making me feel in ways I never thought possible.
As I start to...AWWW!

From that moment on I could no longer accept
that I was Alpha male
'cause you have done to me
what I have done with no other.
I turn to you

Looking you in the eyes.
A pleasant smile covers my face
and I whisper in your ear,
"Jennifer, you are all the man I will ever need."

Yazmín M. Peña

Yazmín M. Peña served as Managing Editor for *Revista de la Academia*, and is the coeditor of *Carlitos Magazine: Start the Change* as well as *The Queer Convention Chapbook*. Her poetry has appeared in *Poetry in Performance*. Yazmín holds an MFA from The City College of New York, and currently works for a national oral history project where she gets to travel all over the continental United States, listening. A Brooklyn resident for the past fifteen years, she still misses her native Dominican Republic and proudly holds the title of "Best Aunt, Ever."

Kink

Curly, wavy, natural (nappy does never apply). Make it kinky. Kinky, Chula, is the way you like it. I'm not fooled by the two hours and a half (if you're lucky) you spend at the salon, colonizing your head.

To break it down: Keep it Safe, Sane always Consensual. Seriously, pay attention. Walking into this Dominican hair salon without speaking Spanish, does not mean you lose your rights. Really, you hold the power...all I do is wield the dryer, you tell me when it's too hot.

Two hours and a half go like this: five minutes on "how you doing?" and "Mija, you're looking good." Two seconds to say "wash-and-set," and then you hand control over. (Negotiations can be a bitch. The secret is to go with hands you already know.)

This is a Dominican place. We will rub you raw, allow the wetness to drip down your neck, between your breasts and into your belly button. You don't need to say you want the deep conditioning: you've given me all control, and with your strands between my fingers, I'll decide if I want to go with the 2 + 1, or just a generic.

An hour under the dryer. The other name of this apparatus is torture. It sucks your tears and the heat tenderizes your scalp. You can attempt to read last month's *Vanidades*, to listen to the bachata reverberating the walls. And yes, I will play the same song over and over again if I feel like it.

Another hour under the blow dryer. I'll stand between your legs, to your side, behind you. I'll booster your follicles, stimulate your roots, if you're a bad girl. If you're a good girl (your gossip is good), I'll slather on a reconstructive Dominican protein treatment before I...

...pull, and pull, blow-dryer and brush dancing back and forth, breasts pressed against your cheek, till every curl has been pressed flat. If the hair is extra shiny, there better be a big tip for me.

This behavior is often referred to as non-normative. I'll make you hurt...you'll thank me. Everyone is a winner.

Fucking You is Like Eating Chimichurris at 4 o'clock in the Morning After a Night Out

Chimichurris (chimis for short)
often called Dominican hamburgers
are made of pork (which I don't eat)
meat cooked on a spit, seasoned, flattened
squeezed between chopped cabbage
drenched in mayonnaise, sliced tomatoes,
red onions (raw), salsa de escabeche and
of course, bread.

The best chimis are at
the street carts, the reddish white sauce
already dripping down your fingers as you take
chimi with one hand, pay with the other,
walk some steps out of the way and bite into
moist, pliable, juicy carne (which I don't eat),
the crispy pan holding it all together,
and you chew not caring that at
four in the morning the sky is already
clearing, your bladder is clamoring for
release, your feet have been trapped
in those heels for so long they've lost
feeling.

You chew and you can almost feel the carne
(which I don't eat) soaking in the rum
and cokes, the vodka tonics and the two shots
of tequila, slowing you down yet waking you up
and you start telling whomever's standing next
to you that if world leaders ate together before
they started talking policy, people would get
along better and damn but chimis are good!

And you chew, chew, messily swallow, your
mouth open without care, eyes semi-closed
every bit of skin cantando,
calories and consequences forgotten
as you go in for another bite.

Chadwick Moore

Chadwick Moore was born in Tennessee and is a 2005 graduate of the University of Iowa Undergraduate Writers Workshop. He's a contributor to the *New York Times* and his work has also appeared in *Out Magazine*, *BUTT*, *Geil*, *K48*, and on *NPR*, among others. He's worked in the editorial departments of Farrar, Straus and Giroux Books in New York City and Black Spring Press in London. He lives in the Bedford-Stuyvesant section of Brooklyn.

On the Nature of Endings

It was a soupy night. A man played the trumpet in the orange streetlight outside the park and cars glided coolly as polite conversation down a deserted Avenue A in New York City's East Village. I saw a drag queen leaning against a brick building on 6th Street, and when she asked me for a cigarette, it felt like the start of an old detective story.

"Are you heading in there?" she asked, indicating the gay bar halfway down the block. "Yeah, me too," she said. I offered my arm to her and we strolled. She looked up at the moon. It was a yellow, whispery moon. She had crammed herself into a python print blazer and a pair of teal pumps. She had short, skinny legs that shimmered in gold tights, a white miniskirt and a studded belt, and she held a red leather clutch against her C-cup breasts that she later told me were sacks of birdseed. Her hair stood a good twelve inches high, a little magenta haystack. She told me it was actually three wigs sewn together.

A few yards away from us, outside the bar, two guys kissed.

"Do you suppose those two are in love?" the drag queen asked.

"Doubtful," I said. They looked like imitations of one another, roughly the same height, both thirty-somethings with dark hair and beards. They were wearing Levi's® and work boots. They were wearing a different kind of drag.

"I think that what most people consider love is such a feeble and restrictive thing," she said. "I laugh when I think about all these guys out looking for boyfriends. There are so many of these people searching. How is it they can't seem to find one another?" She chuckled and shook her head and turned to face me. Her earrings made a pleasing tinkle sound whenever she moved her head. Her eyes had a habit of rolling wearily, like those of some great, dusty mammal. "Just like religion," she said. "To put faith in God is to not have faith in the world. Like, if you love a hope or a belief then you must hate what is real and visible. It's the same thing when people talk about love."

"To expect you'll happen upon another person—simply to believe in the existence of this other person—who will love you and cherish you and make life at once bearable and meaningful—is completely narcissistic in the same way that believing in a God who watches over your shoulder and cares what you do and say is narcissistic."

Standing alongside her made you feel a bit like a dog at the heel of a shepherd. "The Christian resolve to find the world evil and ugly has made the world evil and ugly," she added. "That's Nietzsche." Without being very tall, the height she did have was sudden and unbalanced. She seemed to carry herself in defiance of normal physical laws. Gravity might not have applied to the shape of her hair and the sharpness of her heels and her thin bones. The law that governed her standing before me might be called something like habit. She reminded me of very old mountains found in the Southern Hemisphere that once were fat and rolling but over millennia have been sculpted by the waters of rivers that no longer exist; the kind of otherworldly mountains that don't look like mountains at all, but something more gruesome and decaying—the skeleton of a mountain. The kind with those sharp spires and great, yawning holes cut through the center of them; ancient structures that seem to stand only because somewhere along the way they forgot to tumble down.

"We all want to see ourselves at the center of some great narrative. And love stories," she said, "are fictions based on nothing more than the belief that eventually some perfect person will come along and conveniently end the book. Books and movies end with marriages and deaths because both love and death present illusions of permanence. They are tidy finalities to our individual narratives and they make us feel good. But anyone with half a brain knows that human relationships are as erratic as the beings who compose them. And if we're to believe our relationships will one day reach permanence, that our hearts will find some breezy plateau on which to bask for all of eternity, then we are no longer seeking love. We're seeking something more like social routine. My story will never have two characters and two hearts entangled in a dance. It has only me," she said. "If it's about anything, my story is about money. Or rather a lack of it. Do you know Maugham?"

I told her I did, that he was one of my favorites.

"Good," she said. "Maugham wrote that money is like a sixth sense and without it the others don't function. Money is survival and we can't be content unless we are at least surviving. That's what I've come to realize. That the quest for survival in this fucked-up world generates the only true love there is: it's quiet and contemplative and personal. And any story worth telling is about that kind of love. I have been poor my entire life. I stole these pumps from the thrift store in the basement of the Methodist church in Gramercy Park. I drink a lot." She stamped her cigarette out and dug through her purse for lipstick and a compact mirror. She had a couple of decades on me, at least, and even in heels she wasn't very tall. She had the quality of being both mundane and remarkable at the same time, like a modest tree rising from a vast savannah. "The world is shrewd and underhanded and I am a terribly impractical creature," she admitted. "That's a real love story." Her skin looked chewy and overly tanned and her voice had a nasally, slightly irritating quality.

"For you and me and everyone else there are just four things that are biologically required of us in life." I held her purse while she re-applied her lipstick. "Eating, sleeping, fucking, and breathing. And everything else, if you're lucky, shall be called quite simply love. Remember that," she said, and took her purse back and rubbed her lips together, gave her hair a fluff and her tits a little shimmy. "Or else you'll end up like all these faggots out at the bar every night searching for one another in plain sight."

She walked into the club past the doorman and I followed. Inside was a single, rectangular room with red walls. It was a regulars' bar. I'd been there enough to know that. It was very crowded and very hot. The faces of the people glistened and the air was soppy with the stench of humanity. People were dancing. They'd disposed of the guard on their faces and for a moment appeared strangely amoebic, like nothing but warm shells of liquid and gas bumping up next to one another.

They shuffled silently and mechanically, as though deep inside some unseen force compelled their movements, something beyond their understanding. They closed their eyes and shook their heads. They grabbed each other at the shoulders or at the hips and shifted their weight from side to side, they reached up their arms. They tautly slid their hands down their torsos like creatures shedding old skin. They might've believed themselves the center of some great narrative that had a beginning and an end. And there was, when I looked closer, something else that joined the people here tonight. A particular sallow expression in the face that said their entire existence amounted to little more than a succession of petty dramas and malicious thoughts. There was little else but blind desire amongst them.

Leaning against the bar top we surveyed the room. Clusters of people stood around the periphery, silent and meager looking. I didn't know the song playing. Music like that all sounded the same to me. "Can you believe so many people listen to this bullshit pop music and they actually relate to it?" the drag queen asked. "That this music brings them hope and meaning? If love is the modern opiate, then pop music is its syringe."

The drag queen walked off into the crowd after that and I never saw her again. Four years passed before I thought much about that strange, aging drag queen who took my arm on Avenue A one spring night. I had been out drinking and on my way home picked up one of those free newspapers for the subway ride, the sort of free paper that caters to the anarchist crowd. There inside was a photograph of her. It was a grainy, terribly unflattering snapshot under the headline, "You Will Be Missed, Our Friend Tequila Mockingbird." Seeing her name I felt flushed with humor and tenderness. It was a good drag name. The article said she died about a year ago but the paper just now got word of it. No one knew immediately of her death because she didn't know anyone. The body was found in her apartment in Queens, usual story of the neighbors smelling a foul odor and calling the police. Tequila Mockingbird's carcass was given a city burial service. That's the political way of saying it was cremated along with hundreds of other unclaimed bodies from that year, the ashes tossed in a pine box and buried out on Hart Island in the Bronx, the city graveyard. That's where all those unclaimed bodies go,

800,000 of them so far. A single three-inch placard is laid that states only the year, in this case 2009.

I think the drag queen would have found the whole situation of her death very satisfactory. When I read the article the time was roughly five o'clock in the morning and I was on the subway traversing the Williamsburg Bridge with jagged Brooklyn aglow before me. Raindrops squiggled down the glass. There was not a single person in the world who knew where I was at that very moment. For some reason that thought struck me with a particular force. I began to cry, but not out of sadness. I, like anyone, was just another radical component of the sun rising on yet another day.

There were no fairies in the garden, no saviors on the cross, and no one great love in waiting. We're just here to watch the world spin, and spin the world shall. The drag queen said love only ends the story in books and movies. And as for death, we can't be certain if death's the end of the story since no one who's experienced it has been able to report back to us. Perhaps a moment such as this is always how the story begins and will end. Perhaps this moment is where the camera pans out and the disco beat rises. This is where the audience cheers and the screen fades to black. This is where you're once again sitting on a train, alone. But this version of an ending, like all endings, relies very heavily on the rest of the story being implied.

Claudia Narváez-Meza

Claudia Narváez-Meza is a lesbian, Mahayana Buddhist, and clinical social worker born in Managua, Nicaragua, and raised in Williamsburg, Brooklyn. She received her M.F.A. in Creative Writing from Brooklyn College and her M.S.W. from New York University. Her writing appears in the Latina lesbian issue of *Sinister Wisdom* and the anthology, *Homelands: Women's Journeys Across Race, Place, and Time*. Claudia currently works as a trauma recovery clinician with children and adolescents at the New York Society for the Prevention of Cruelty to Children. She is also a therapist at the Institute for Human Identity, providing individual and couple therapy for the lesbian, gay, bisexual, and transgender community.

viernes silencioso

for my wife

Shoulder of a cayenne sky
slips in between us
where we lay
hours after lovemaking
lucid harmony of hands

my cheek to your hipbone
temple of my beginning
my ear to ocean's violet tide
outside our window
where iridescent blue
cleaves at our sleep
your breath stirring

you murmur into the pillow
reach for me in sleep
your brown back a shifting delta
beneath purple symmetries
of dewy leaves

I am humbled in this vigil
over your dreaming head
knowing the moon's pull
as waves heave their bodies
against the jagged teeth of rocks.

Fusions

Before the rains spun light
in oral dance
flushed crimson
the urge to enter her

milk threads
this season of merging
past the bones of her mothers
muscled fusions
pulses the drum
pound liquid

her pearl at my lip

raw mouth
oscillates in velvet
I spread sacred
her secret oils
milk cooling
in brief transparencies

thighs that crown me

tomorrow I wake
void of her
the year is human again.

una tarde en domingo

She is the country that salts my skin,
belly's cave collapsing where we merge
secretly these mouths of unwritten
rivers, dried sage, crushed cloves, coco
milk of her cloistered heat where I go
seeking, she is cooling mercury
tempered in coral, young cedar after
rains have given their song, the laughing
falcon at the heights of Momotombo,
madre de cacao, wing of an orange-
chinned parakeet, my palo de sal, she is
the Inca dove turtle perishing in fishnets,
the taro leaf and black laurel country
from which I draw this name, I am
learning to finally yield.

Roberto F. Santiago

Roberto F. Santiago writes placing pen to paper and fingertips to QWERTY as an act of translation. Within poetry he has discovered a booming collective of voices and a rickety soapbox for his multiple identities whereupon he can shout obscenities and prayers at the same time. Currently, Roberto is teaching English Composition as well as working on his MFA at Rutgers University. Travel has also greatly influenced Roberto as a poet. Be it sitting on the grass at Dauchau and staring into the sun or the smell of rain in rural Québec, he has begun to rewrite his own passport. Roberto also writes and produces music and has been known to dance until he rips his pants. He is a New Yorican Bronx native who has accumulated over twenty addresses to date.

And Then We Kissed

It was bound to happen.
Two shapes dancing
across from each other, near each other, against each other.
Our friends continually becoming smoke
breaks somewhere above ground. We were the only people there.
The subtle punctuation and retreat of inner wrists
exposing pulses racing down
the blue highways of Ginsu arms
cutting through the twinkled disco ball strobing
each time 'your song' comes on.
Tonight, every song has been yours.
The way you toss your head back,
as if you were so far out of reach
pretending not to notice me touching
and tugging the elastic advertisement
on your soft bronze, your belly-button
and the smooth line that leads my hands nowhere
the shirtless boys can see.
There is a letterboxing of the moment when our chests touch.
Belt buckles tangle. Foreheads meet. Noses Eskimo.
Your smile is the difference between light and neon.
I lick your breath from my lips.

Carrier

Laying there unconscious, he crosses
my threshold. The skin around my lips
tightens. San Andreas, my hairline,
a line of fault,
pushed apart, my thoughts
are exposed negatives.
He thinks I am going straight
to hell. He lives in Tampa.
He's a born-again Christian
and (he was) my first.
With two hands
two times bigger than mine,
he tears small beating ventricles from their chambers
and molds them
into flightless birds that breathe smog,
grey and lost. He promised me Orion's belt
and tonight, lasso in hand
he will deliver. A message written on broken latex.
Elastic around ankle. I leap
pointlessly outstretched, amongst gilded palms.
I don't want to get over him,
My bones love him. His face fits
into phantom limbs. A neat collection
of lashes, marrow and sea water.
I could see the kids in San Juan jumping off the bridge
into the area rocosa in his Capia gold eyes.
He had never seen snow before.
He wore his brown leather chanclas
Rain or shine. He said he wanted to feel the cold air.
For him, I never wash my hands.

Say Yes

When he's not home
I can be. Filling the dent.
Keeping his side warm.
I understand you love him
but I don't want that for us.
I just want to explore
the way you hug me for that extra second
warmly exhaling behind my right ear
softly grazing your bottom lip against the cologne I wear
that drives you to think about the times we sit together
accidentally bumping into each other
under the table. A match brushing against its book.
Over and over. I long to extend
those small eternities when you laugh and touch my forearm for
longer than you should. The way you blush
when I touch your waist as I walk past.
That static feeling of skin.
I'm not asking you for anything
you don't already want.
I am simply stating my availability.
On the side. Lined up. That last shot before you head home.
Filled with that warm, smoky oakbarrel-aged courage
that asks for my number under flickering neon.
Weekends and evenings
just make a few of those hours mine.
I can be all the things
he used to be
before the ring,
before the politics, domesticity.
He can have the holidays, family dinners, mops and brooms
I just want the night. The sounds you make and the space
where your spine bows inward. Where my chest fits.
Pressed against.

Maegan Ortiz

Maegan "La Mamita Mala" Ortiz is a Queens, New York City-born and bred single mami, poeta, blogger, freelance writer, activista, and twitterputa. For the past five years she has helped edit VivirLatino.com, featuring commentary on Latino politics and culture. Her political writings, poetic puterías y otras desmadres have gotten her to say "presente" in the *SPEAK! Radical Women of Color* spoken-word CD, *make/shift*, *Latina*, *HITN*, the *New York Daily News*, *NPR*, HISPANIC PANIC!, *A.M. NY*, and, most recently, at El Museo del Barrio. She lives with her two hijas in Casa Mala in a land called the mami'hood nestled somewhere between Bayamón y Bushwick and broadcasts her puterías at lamamitamala.com and on Twitter (@mamitamala).

Oración a la santísima chocha

Tú, concha de Yemayá, con perla de Ochún
Ruega por nosotras
Boca de fuego que sangra magma panal en la boca de amantes
Formando ríos de aguas dulces que caen de labios.
Ruega por nosotros
Llave de vida con perfume viajero
Ruega por nosotras
Alimentación ardiente de dedos, penes, y bocas
Ruega por nosotras
Perdóname por dejar tanto tiempo pasar
Tanto tiempo, demasiado de tiempo
Sin que unas lenguas corren por el Laberinto de mi labia
Mapa de mundos
Ruega por nosotras
Sirena peluda
Ruega por nosotras
Cueva de placeres
Ruega por nosotras
Campo de batalla
Ruega por nosotras
Sobreviviente que brilla con magnificencia
Ruega por nosotras
Ciclo de luna
Ruega por nosotras
Espuma roja del mar
Ruega por nosotras
Que sigues bendiciendo al mundo con tu dulzura
Santísima chocha
Ampáranos
Amen

Larry La Fountain-Stokes

Larry La Fountain-Stokes is a Puerto Rican writer, performer, and scholar. Born and raised in San Juan, Puerto Rico, he received his bachelor's degree from Harvard in 1991 and a doctorate in Spanish from Columbia University in 1999. He is currently an Associate Professor of American Culture and Romance Languages and Literatures at the University of Michigan, Ann Arbor, where he specializes in Latina/o, Puerto Rican and Hispanic Caribbean studies, with additional interests in women's, gender, and sexuality studies; lesbian, gay, and queer studies; and theater and performance. He is author of *Queer Ricans: Cultures and Sexualities in the Diaspora* (University of Minnesota Press, 2009), which focuses on Puerto Rican LGBT migration and culture, and of a book of short stories called *Uñas pintadas de azul/Blue Fingernails* (Bilingual Press/Editorial Bilingüe, Arizona, 2009). He was one of the co-editors of a special issue of *CENTRO: Journal of the Center for Puerto Rican Studies* on Puerto Rican Queer Sexualities (2007). He regularly teaches courses on Latina/o literature, culture, and cinema.

la mierda (shit)

He was afraid to begin the story by talking about shit, but his fear proved to be ill founded. And why not? For Hans (whom everyone knew as Juan) got home as fast as he could but it was already too late: he had started to shit in his pants, like a broken, irrepressible dam, and his feces sprayed forward like a dark, premature ejaculation. It was bitterly cold that terrible night in which all of our worst possible nightmares began: my fear of censorship, the moment in which disgust will consume us all, both you and me, before the worms begin to feast on that rotting flesh that hangs off of our bones, those half-disintegrated belongings that we excrete day after day without thinking twice. It is the secret longing that causes fear, I think. But I don't want to jump the gun.

He ran down the street in vain, unable to control himself. Shame compounded his despair, the impossibility of not doing anything. Similar episodes had always ended otherwise. His disgust provoked tears, but dear readers, don't feel pity beforehand. Disgust shall soon be yours too, disgust for the sake of art, and the pleasure of a tiny chocolate of the highest quality, Lady Godiva no less—just in case, just like in the fairy tales you've undoubtedly heard. The presence of shit is the mystery that concerns me. And who guarantees that it was not his fault, or that he did not enjoy it?

"Shit!" he said loudly, as he accidentally passed his dirty hand over his mouth. Accidentally, he would like to say. But I can't lie, I can't, my ears burn red just from thinking about it, and it even makes me blush. Let us change the topic, shall we? He ran down the street, I don't know why, but it was late and infernally cold.

Fortunately, one of his father's alcoholic attacks came to mind, as if to distract him. Memory offered certain rescue strategies. It went like this: a friend of his had organized an exhibit about recycling, and his father started to scream that that was a joke, that nothing worked in Puerto Rico.

"Local politics on this island ruin everything. Let them loose and those government assholes will screw it up," he said.

Juan's father had a notoriously bad Austro-Hungarian temperament that always got worse after drinking rum and mint schnapps, clean and refreshing like a glass of Cuban mojito or like a good tube of strong toothpaste, a most suitable antiseptic for emphysema-ridden throats poorly accustomed to the tropics. Didn't I tell you he'd digress? All because of solid waste, because of a corrupt family history! Between alcohol and shit, a regular chip off the old block. Running down the street in the cold, he can hardly wait for things to get better and he almost stumbles but manages to get back together before suddenly falling backwards in a sewer.

Among their other hysterias, Juan's parents had a campaign against disposable diapers, because of their expense and non-biodegradable nature. "You always broke out in a rash when we tried to put them on you, Juan," his mother piped up. "That's why we always used one hundred percent cotton." His father then explained that to get rid of the child's crap they would place the diaper in the toilet. That is exactly what he would do with his soiled underwear. The main fear was that it would start to trickle down his leg, reaching his shoes; that he would stain the elevator floor—that he'd have to go clean it up later. Fortunately, his Hanes® withstood. He was thankful that he was wearing briefs and not boxers that day, or worse, nothing, like a certain time he had gone to the gym without a clean replacement. Sexy, but rather impractical. I'm sure some of you will know that rather well.

He had already received calls in the past, inquiring if he had soiled underwear, stained with the crust of his offal. He used to leave phone messages on a sex line. He had doubted whether to do it that night; he hadn't been very successful lately. He was tired of having the hours pass by with no calls, uselessly waiting by the phone and growing more frustrated. But then Tony rang him up. Or perhaps it was another day, in another city, far, far away: they met, went to an empty apartment which he was remodeling, and did what he was told. His name was Ronnie (well, all right, Ronaldo, like the Brazilian soccer star) and his face was a vague memory of days gone by, always cloudy and full of icy frost. Ronaldo was a workman as well, a carpenter, in fact.

While the nausea consumed him, Juan thought, humorously, "I wish that motherfucker would call me today!" He cleaned himself carefully, and after removing a small crustacean formation, suddenly smelled the sea. He quickly opened the bathroom window, letting the salt air in, a strong scent of mangroves, something from his transatlantic memory, a wasting syndrome or mystical trance. "I wish I had matches," thinking of sulfur and candles, an ex-boyfriend's trick against the stench. The sea worshipped him, but in vain, amidst so many tall cement and brick buildings. As if two men, one first (in the imagination, I would say) and another one in the flesh.

Tony was a construction worker and sweated a lot but didn't care for showers or deodorant or clean clothes. Quite the contrary, he grew excited from having his odoriferous muscled body worshipped as is, smelly and sort of filthy, blindfolded, with stained underwear filling his mouth, a pissed and masturbated jock strap covering his nostrils. Hans found it alluringly sexy but also intimidating. Tony is a figment of his imagination, a phone call and nothing more, but Ronaldo will make him see the stars, except that stars don't smell well, they are scary and hurt. Once you realize that he who has done it tells another tale, another story; he who touches the flesh knows, plays pool in a lesbian bar anticipating the climactic moment that is about to come. He who has tasted shit and thrown up is grateful, because the stars of the sky shine that much more strongly in your eyes once you stick your tongue in and taste its foul nature. Because he makes you a woman but then asks you to fuck him up the ass. That's the part I don't understand, the greatest mystery, but for these explanations, get a philosopher.

"Do you wanna come over to my house?" he said.

"All right," the other one responded, his voice quivering ever so slightly.

"I don't think this is really your scene."

"I just like talking to you over the phone."

"Do you have dirty underwear? Go get them," he insisted, somewhat aggressively, like a general in command.

Hans didn't know what to do, he didn't want to lie. Truth is, that day he had no dirty underwear, and Tony wanted really filthy ones. At any rate, what self-respecting Puerto Rican pansy would have soiled bottoms lying around for a long time, even if he lived like a stylish dandy in New York, in exile thousands of miles away from his mother? Especially one who had descended from such noble blood, son of the choicest Austro-Hungarian families and of a lovely Rumanian countess who fled to the Caribbean with her servant! Of course, while they spoke, he masturbated. In fact, everything started to seem more attractive over the phone, more—how should I say—appealing. He would have said "delectable" if he hadn't been so afraid (or perhaps felt some other, less stereotyped emotion), a fear of wetting his lips at that moment, of kneeling and taking the boots off the man who will soon abuse you. But you know what, fuck fear. And when you throw up, he will tell you to spit in the corner but later forget about it.

As a child, Juan would run from his bedroom to the small bathroom in the back of the house, especially at night. Perhaps his father, drunk once again, had fallen asleep on the toilet up front, with a cigarette in his lips or his hand slowly burning a hole in the green polyester bathroom rug. The small hot bathroom–el bañito—would provoke claustrophobia, an asphyxiating perspiration, although it was also somewhat safe and comforting. The mirrored medicine chest held all of his cousin's theater makeup, from the days of her high school thespian career. She was a whitish diva from Miramar, deadly cousin of Pre-Raphaelite cadavers such as the ones his grandfather collected in his doctor's office in Mayagüez. The cousin was, just like him, a Creole version of Germans and Austro-Hungarians and had a bit of malice in her stare, like a hornet's stinger that she could fire at the slightest provocation. But is this of any interest at all to your man?

Childhood defecations in the small bathroom hurt so much that Juancito imagined that he was giving birth. That was his punishment, the painful menstruation that he would never have—the dark feces instead of blood. It was an unimaginable pain that could only be understood as the result of a diet rich in canned foods and devoid of fiber or fresh substance. Everything was canned: the juice for breakfast, the preserved fruits in sugary syrup in the afternoon, the bland and tasteless evening vegetables. Everything accompanied by roasted meats and boiled potatoes, schnitzel, knockwurst, sauerkraut, greasy milk, mustard, dreary pale lettuce lacking any chlorophyll. American cheese and soft drinks. Moldy fruits that arrived on slow ships, with second-rate produce sent to abandoned colonies such as his as if they were banished in outer space in a prison colony with Sigourney Weaver, fearing the attack of a formidable, horrific creature. The dismembered body of who knows whom, torn apart by a gigantic, industrial fan. Did he feel the same?

The little bathroom is where they went when a girl stuck gum in his hair, gum that his mother had to mercilessly hack away at with scissors in order to remove. But had it been him, or one of his blonde sisters? Who the victim? Who the perpetrator? Scissors, gum, makeup that distracted him often enough, perhaps not the same day as the pains, but another, the day he circled his nipples with that greasy beige lipstick that was so hard to remove. A thick, greasy paint, while he hallucinated about letting his almost-white hair grow to his waist and making two thick braids like Lady Godiva's. Then he would paint his face with drawings that looked more like an Apache or a Taíno. Or, if not, with burnt cork, to make himself look like a jíbaro, just as he did for costume parties at Casa de España! An Austro-Hungarian jíbaro from a ruined family come to less in a hot but very clean Antillean island.

Overwhelmed by the heinous stench, Hans carefully started to take his clothes off and let them fall in the hallway, anywhere. He moved the bath mat and got into the shower, where he took off his pants and made the unpleasant transfer to the toilet. Alas, his feces-covered buttocks dripped here and there. The temporary relief provoked by his sidewalk, hallway, and elevator intestinal liberation was accompanied by other sudden discharges in the apartment. When he sat, without thinking and certainly unwillingly, he smeared the toilet seat, which he later had to clean. He started the shower and bathed, but the water and soap, which in other circumstances always provoked great pleasure, could barely wash away the memory of his pain.

It had not been an unexpected attack. It had all started when, short moments after finishing his dinner, he had felt a sharp pain in his gut, a clear sign that something was amiss. The tanks advanced slowly down the streets of his domains, soldiers with lascivious looks of evil in their eyes: "Long live the Fatherland!" his stomach seemed to growl. On the way home, he once again felt uncomfortable rumblings. "It's the Gestapo's fault," he thought, "I have been poisoned!" It was unbearably cold, he wanted to get home as soon as possible and believed that he would make it. "Luftwaffe flyers, pink triangles searching for an innocent victim!" The planes threatened to drop their bombs at any moment, as if he had swallowed Argentine beef, the memory of an animal that had died in agony after a grass-induced indigestion.

In fact, a greasy Chinese meal was at the root of his unfortunate ordeal. His German-Caribbean stomach betrayed him with such cruelty so frequently, although never before in such a dramatic fashion. Over-seasoned broccoli in brown sauce; deep-fried deveined shrimp bathed in chili peppers and Oriental spices; a sudden bodily release akin to death, a piercing similar to a burnt hole in a green synthetic rug which could have let anything into his body, some virus, who knows, a trance. If diarrhea was the first sign, the letter of introduction, the painful wound, a certain letter of invitation to a party one didn't really want to go to but was obliged to attend. A party where they would play hallucinating Mozart waltzes or something by Schumann, or by Wagner, perhaps. To say *E. coli* is to say it all. The diarrhea that awaited him every day, while he said the rosary, a symptom that he knew would be the first sign. The intestinal decomposition he had all the time (septicemia?), but that he had always kept inside until reaching the bathroom. Tony's release—provoked with Ex-Lax®?

The thing is that with Ronaldo, it was a completely different story, one of nausea, but Ronaldo really plays no role in this episode. Ronaldo is the memory of a disgusting future yet to come which will make you hallucinate for the rest of your days, the pain of a burnt back from fucking on the hard rug of a kitchen under construction. Intertwining the powerful ambience of magical trances, a certain *je ne sais quoi* of the mind. Swallow Ronaldo, let him out, it is the tongue that speaks and that knows the flavor.

"Can't you ask him?" the doctor asks, but you say no.

It is true. Oh, tragic cruelty of a soulless life that does not forgive one small fault regardless of how minuscule or brief! The illusions of a foul-smelling phone call never consummated, like a certain dangerous skinhead that Hans met over the internet another day who smelled just as bad as Tony but also had a swastika tattooed on his forearm, supposedly just for shock value. And just think, the poop of a child who only drinks mother's milk comes out yellow, pure, odorless, but why think? Certainly without an unpleasant smell, nighttime extends itself interminable in her gaze, choking in his throat, the fear awaiting! And the thought that his shit smelled like the end of the world according to Wim Wenders. Whatever happened to his childhood poop? Winged, flying through the skies of Berlin, as if it really mattered, slightly more than anything else. His baby poop, packed away with his first tiny red-headed German curls of very strawberry-blond hair, so pretty, so white, which he seemed to be losing as time went by. He was about to turn thirty and was afraid of the future, as he certainly should be, you say. Only fools fear nothing.

But it was precisely the reaction of his friend that interested him, that drove him mad and made him fail at being a good son of the nation. How many of our race have lost themselves down such roads and scandals of the dark life? Hans called Anthony again to talk, twenty-five cents, or was it from his house? He had the worst intentions; undoubtedly, he must have read diabolical treatises to get such evil thoughts, something by the Countess of Merlin, or perhaps Huysmans or Martha Stewart, desirous of redecorating the house in pastel tones as if for the Marquis de Sade. I tell you, people just do not cooperate nowadays, much less follow God's word. Look at what has happened with the tithe.

"Hi, how are you?" our precocious criminal said, in full knowledge of his intent to commit such a nefarious act that no mortal author could have previously fathomed on the face of this earth.

"Good. What's up?" Tony replied, clueless about the transformation his peer had undergone.

"Nothing new. Do you like bloody underwear? I have hemorrhoids," Hans confessed, in ecstasy. He neglected to mention Ronaldo, not to spoil the surprise, and because it was irrelevant.

Always wanting to be a woman, and it came to him the day he least expected, during a little trip to learn about his lost Argentinean roots. He went to the bathroom, took a dump, and noticed a bright red stain on the toilet paper after he wiped. The more he rubbed, the more he bled. He got up concerned and immediately called a female friend.

"Don't worry, it's normal. It happens to many people," she responded, but said nothing else.

Truth of the matter is that people wash their hands just to look good. But make no mistake—since he was so fond of rimming, he made sure to brush his teeth well before going out to the bars in Recoleta and San Telmo. Then, suddenly, he started to notice dark stains on his underwear and on occasions, even on his pants. He stopped eating empanadas on the street even though he liked them and he tried to only drink bottled water and soda. He also stopped eating hot, spicy condiments and greasy foods. It got better after a couple of days—perhaps the K-Y explorations were like an internal massage, as people love to say, but I've read otherwise. They all think you bleed because of the rape, but it is exactly the opposite, my dear. Ronaldo keeps quiet but that is because sometimes silence says far more than words.

It is a real shame that he did not learn from his mistakes, like a hummingbird that gets skewered on the fangs of a miniature vampire in the flowered gardens of Dante's hell. Hans—I mean Juan—seemed to have inherited a touch of his progenitor's alcoholism. But no, that was not the case at all. Rather, he was fraught with anger and unsolved anxieties that made him an unhappy mess of a man. "Who would have thought that the inheritor of such noble lineage would do such things?" people in the know would gossip for days. The list of landowners in Miramar is notoriously long in its weaknesses and claims of infamy; it stretches out a thousand miles towards the horizon and is stained with blue blood, all noble, like the odorless poop of a baby. Alcoholism would have been a noble response to his loneliness and constipation (or rather, his diarrhea) which led him down such treacherous paths. A straight line that did not lead to a well known place, but rather to an ominous secret full of needles and white powder. Strange that he should end up falling into that, such a good boy, but one never knows. He lost all inhibitions and started to feel much, much, much better, free as a bird, too free some would say. But what do they know?

Anthony begged him to come over right away.

Juan didn't want to speak any longer, but he was happy. He threw up on his face by mistake (damn gag reflex) and then they fucked until exhaustion. The drug thing was all a lie, but that is the only untruth in this whole story, I swear on my mother's grave! The light of morning was starting to filter into the room, and he was suddenly grateful for having left that message in spite of all the unpleasantly delightful episodes we all endured. Tony closed the curtains and they fell asleep, cuddling like babies. And we all know that there is no greater pleasure than to rest with your lover after having committed the nefarious act.

This would be a lovely ending if it wasn't for the fact that it was missing one crucial detail (Anthony, a female friend in Buenos Aires whom he calls because he doesn't know what to do, the history of recycling in Puerto Rico and his friend who knows so much about garbage and zafacones). But Ronaldo's story is different, among falsified family trees and other confusions, and I can't tell it right now, at least not today, because of my rather serious professional limitations. Can't you see that it is always preferable to look from the outside so that one remains invisible? Ronaldo undoes everything that is ever told, he transforms it, lets my vain cleanliness become real, as hard as I try to avoid it. It is sad but true and I will most likely go to the grave with his secret, which I never tire of repeating. This is the way it goes. Shit spreads over the horizon because my throat is multifaceted, everything goes down, I always swallow everything for your love, my little alelí blossom, my everlasting Teocalli de Cholula.

Pietro Scorsone

Pietro Scorsone is a New York City-born artist. His writing has appeared in the *Other Rooms Press Journal* and he's had his music reviewed in the *Village Voice*. Pietro's mission in life is to inspire mass acts of cannibalism, political dissent, and spontaneous outbreaks of choreographed musical numbers.

God in an Alcove

Perfect is perfect and perfection is to be observed, admired, and consumed. Perfection should never be allowed to go to waste. Never tolerate its destruction. Never envy it.

Porcelain. Alabaster. Dissolved into the wall behind him. Camouflage.

An eyeball that looks like a marble miniature of the earth. Lips always on the verge of a kiss, even when speaking. Detached from his face, those lips, they still looked alive.

Everything he did was a testament to nature. Snow White with birds landing on her finger. Top of the class; fastest on the track. But if you gave him a reason to be sad, he'd do that perfectly. His sadness was beautiful.

I punished him with his own DNA. A funhouse mirror for the soul. We shared a shell. But his was just better and no one could explain how. Our fingers, our toes, our cocks, all so alike. But his were perfect. Identical twins no one ever mistook for one another. I never envied him; I just wanted us to be alike.

I first showed him the depths of our living room alcove as children. You'd never notice the passage behind Jesus and Mary. Like protectors of the gate, they stood on the ledge keeping your eye from seeing into the tunnel that led to the heart of our house. It was built in the 1800s by a French mystic architect. On each floor, two rooms had alcoves with doors and crawl spaces in the back leading to a room you'd never think was there.

By the time we moved into the house all the tunnels had been walled off, except the one in the living room. The hidden room was tall enough to stand in, maybe big enough for four people to make a circle. From the other rooms in the house you could never tell it was there, or taking up any space. Our father was supposed to have walled up the living room passage, but forgot when I hung the shawl behind Jesus and Mary.

I found the room, cleaned it, and left a flashlight inside. At first we would just play with soldiers in there, its ominous darkness befit the trials of combat. As we grew older, it became the room of truth.

He walked with such an air of life about him. We'd walk home from school. The same friends, the same smiles, the same voice, our words were alike. The only grief he felt was when he started to notice mine. His empathy let me in. Where I needed to be. Inside him. That was when the room of truth began. He wanted to talk to me, to know what was bothering me. When I lied, he created the rule. In that room, he said, you can't lie, or the spirit of the mystic architect will take you. I laughed, and followed him in, behind Jesus, behind Mary, on all fours, crawling. We each sat in a corner, facing each other, dirty knees bent. Matching blue and red striped sport socks below Our Lady of Pompeii gym shorts.

Tell me the truth.

You hurt me, I said. You're perfect.

But you're the same as me. We're exactly the same.

No, everything about you is just a little different.

Well then let's change me. We need to be the same.

Empathy.

His concept of our existence was different than mine. He saw the physical, the embryo splitting to make two identical beings, but I saw the One splitting to make Two Halves. Two very different halves.

I thought if his insides, his soul, matched mine, his outsides would disfigure accordingly. I tried to convince him he had all the things I hated about myself inside him. I told him about the rage, the misguided passions—all the thoughts that took me away from his happy butterfly world. But he had an answer for everything. Nothing shook him but his awareness of my pain.

Outside we had soccer, baseball, friends, and arcades; parents that loved us and appreciated our need for pizza. Who wanted it?

By that summer, right after our first high school birthday party, the room became our everything. The blankets that now lined its floor stank like our sweat. It was always ninety degrees in there. We made up social events to cover the hours we spent in the room of truth, trying to be one person.

I think it's everything around us that makes us wrong. Mom and Dad treat us like different people. Teachers do too.

I know, why the fuck can't they just let us be you or me?

Don't you feel like when we're in here we get closer and closer to it?

Are you kidding? We're almost there. I can feel it.

Speaking of feeling it...

I laughed.

That summer we had started a new tradition. We sat in the room naked. Aside from the heat, we felt it made us more pure. More honest. The sweat made it all the more cleansing. Before we'd get dressed and climb out through the passage, we'd jerk off. Neither of us proposed the idea, it just made sense. We'd shoot into our hands, then rub our cummy palms together. Each time we became more and more one.

We need to get rid of everything around us. All the influences. Right? Just us alone, we could be just me or you.

We should be just you. This is all yours. You made us close enough to get here.

So let's do it tonight.

I love you, he said.

I love us, too.

We sat at dinner, as happy as we'd ever been. We talked to Mom and Dad about making state finals and maybe going into the city to see Duran Duran. I went to the bathroom and took out ten of Mom's valium and crushed them up.

We'll clear the plates—do you guys want some more wine?

While they relaxed at the table we put the dishes in the washer and mixed the valium into the glasses we refilled. We told them how we discovered *Pitfall* didn't actually have an end. It didn't matter which direction you went in above ground or below. We played and played until one of us got so far the timer ran out. And that was it. Done. They looked at us blankly. Mom got tired, told us she loved us, and they went to bed.

Get the toolbox.

I got it. Do you have the lantern fuel?

It's in the garage, be right back.

Ok, I'll start the rounds.

We locked all the doors and windows and closed all the curtains, starting from downstairs. We went to Mom and Dad's bedroom. She was asleep in bed; he was passed out on the floor. We dragged him in bed with her and poured the fluid all over them. We threw a match, and watched the blaze begin. They slept soundly under the burning bed sheet.

Quick, let's get to the room of truth, we don't have much time.

And we crawled, toolbox in tow, into the alcove. As soon as we got in the room we undressed and kissed for the first time.

I'm ready to be you.

We rolled on the blankets, rubbing and kissing and sweating, as the temperature rose. He put his legs on my shoulders and I slid down to his cock. He tasted perfect, as only he could. I sucked him up and down and licked him from his asshole to his balls. Perfect. I took one in my mouth and bit down. Hard. He never screamed, he just said I love you. I bit and gnawed as hard as I could until it came off in my mouth, sack and all. I swallowed it and moved on to the other.

I love you, he said.

I love us, too.

The blood flowed down into his ass crack, where I had lined myself up. I started fucking. He pulled my head down and kissed me voraciously. Tears streamed from both our eyes, burning from the sweat and love as the temperature kept rising. I took his lower lip in my mouth and sucked and ripped it off and spit it out beside me. Then I took his other lip.

I love us.

Crying, I pulled out of him and licked at his cock head while jerking him off. A blood gargle and a whimper and he came in my mouth. I swallowed that, too. I took a blade from the toolbox and cut the erection from his body. I felt it go limp in my hand, as the blood left from its stem. I swallowed it whole with blood from his crotch to ease the way down. My skin felt like it was burning; the heat was perfect and disorienting.

I was back inside him, fucking. I used a widget from the toolbox to pull out each of his eyeballs. I ingested one and put the other on the floor next to his lips. I kissed what was left of his mouth, pulled out and stopped myself from coming. I grabbed his lips.

Detached from his face, those lips, they still looked alive.

I placed his eye in the corner and pointed it directly at us. There were sounds of crackling and crashing coming from each passage attached to the room. The smoke started entering with authority, as I started jerking off. Staring into my brother's eye I came in my hand, all over his lips, and I kissed them and swallowed them—and the eye.

I love you, he said.

I could hear his voice in my head. Guiding my way out the passage, as the room collapsed behind me; through the doorway. The Jesus and Mary fell out of my way as I reached the alcove. The voice told me where to crawl, to find our way out. It was our voice.

We crawled off the porch and across the lawn. Lying on our back, we thought about how we corrected a mistake; took two halves, a fractured soul, and brought them together. We created a new life.

We listened to the neighbors gathering around us; the oh my gods and what should we dos. Sirens getting louder by the second. And we felt semen leak onto our stomach, from our spent cock, cooling the burning skin. We were perfect.

Charles Rice-González

Charles Rice-González was born in Puerto Rico, reared in the Bronx, and is a writer, long-time community and LGBT activist, and Executive Director of BAAD!, The Bronx Academy of Arts and Dance. His work has been published in *The Pitkin Review*, *Los Otros Cuerpos* (the first anthology of Puerto Rican queer writing), *Best Gay Stories 2008,* and in the upcoming *Kweli Journal* and *Ambientes: New Queer Latino Writing* edited by Lázaro Limas and Felice Picano. He received a B.A. in Communications from Adelphi University and an M.F.A. in Creative Writing from Goddard College. His debut novel, *Chulito,* about a tough, sexy hip hop-loving, young Latino man, coming out and coming of age in the South Bronx, will be published in 2011. He's working on his second novel, *Hunts Point*, a look at a South Bronx neighborhood through a queer Latino lens, and will co-edit a gay Latino fiction anthology with fellow scribe Charlie Vázquez, *From Macho to Mariposa: New Gay Latino Fiction* (working title) due spring 2011.

Hallelujah Pow! (excerpt from *Chulito*)

Chulito kept dozing off and waking up whenever a truck sped by or some loud talking guys coming home from a night out passed the car. But the next time he opened his eyes the newly risen Sunday morning sun shined brightly across the sky. Chulito had just become a Saturday night leftover as he waited for 'Kaze to come back from "talking" to Brenda.

He looked at the car clock: 7:37AM. The storefronts down on Garrison and Hunts Point Avenues had their metal gates shut tight as eyelids. There was no one in the street: no trucks, no auto glass guys, just a few well-dressed churchgoers in the distance. Carlos was probably asleep in his bed. Chulito remembered their first trip to the Village, their first kiss in Poe Cottage, and the way Carlos almost cried when he came. Chulito slipped into a warm ocean of memories when he heard a distant thunderous roar: "Hallelujaaaaaah!" The second "Hallelujah" was louder and shook Chulito from his dream. He looked out through the tinted windows of Kamikaze's car and saw that Rivera's bodega had opened and Chin-Chin and Looney Tunes were standing in front of it. Looney Tunes, who had been talking on the pay phone, stopped and looked around a little puzzled. A woman pushing a baby carriage stood on the corner waiting for the light to change and she, too, looked around. The time on the clock car read 9:56AM. Just as the woman was about to cross the street, a third loud, "Haaaaalleluuuujaaaaah," rose like a battle cry and the front doors of the three churches on Manida Street burst open and out poured an army of born-again Christians. They were dressed in their simple, fine church clothes and held phonebook-sized bibles over their heads as if they were protecting themselves from a rainfall of sin. Their heels clicked on the sidewalks as they headed down Manida Street toward Garrison Avenue. Chulito sat up and watched the charge of the Christians coming toward him. A fourth Hallelujah rose to the sky. Through the car's tinted windows, Chulito could see throngs of Christians running full speed toward him from the churches down Garrison Avenue. The woman pushing the baby carriage ran across the street toward Rivera's bodega, where Looney Tunes and Chin-Chin stood frozen in awe of the mob headed their way.

The Christians from Manida Street split when they got to Garrison Avenue. Half of them went to the right and met up with a huge crowd coming along Garrison. The other half went to the left and ran past Kamikaze's car. Their faces were red with righteousness and the men, women, and even children, held on to their bibles as they continued to charge.

The mob swarmed around the guys on the corner and yelled, "Sinners! Repent from your evil ways. Accept Jesus Christ as your personal savior." Looney Tunes barked back, "Fuck you! Get away from me!" A tall Latino man swung his bible and hit Looney on the side of his head. Looney Tunes fell to the ground. "What the fuck?"

"Now do you accept Jesus?" The man raised his bible as Looney Tunes crouched down on the sidewalk silent. The man hit him again. Looney Tunes tried to get up and run, but a group of young men and women grabbed him. "Do you accept Jesus as your personal savior?" Looney Tunes was disoriented and bruised. He spit out blood and received repeated strikes from the man and from several other Christians near him. Another man posed the same question to Chin-Chin. "Yes! Yes! I do!" His acceptance was met with a resounding hallelujah and about eight men and women scooped him off the ground, held him high in the air, and charged toward one of the churches on Manida Street. All around similar scenes were happening. "Accept Christ?" "No." Pow! There were people lying bloodied in the street, while others were being carried into the churches. The woman, her baby and the baby carriage were all en route to a church via a group of Christians. The mob had stopped delivery trucks, buses and cars, and posed the same question; affirmatives were met with cheers.

A van suddenly screeched to a halt about two feet from Chulito. It had bumper stickers that read "God is Awesome," "Christ rocks," and "Choose Jesus or Die." The door slid open and about 15 young men in dark purple shiny suits carrying bibles with hard covers made of metal stormed out. They had headsets on and joined the crusading Christians. Similar vans arrived and more young Christians came out and joined the crowd. One man got on top of one of the vans, put a bullhorn to his mouth, and started preaching, "My brothers and sisters, we offer you a choice for a new life today. Stop your evil ways and come to Christ." He burst into tears. "Oh people! Jesus loves you, can't you see?" And he fell to his knees on top of the van. "Come to Jesus, stop the drugs, the sex and disease. Clean your lives not only for your own good, but for the good of the whole neighborhood and the world. Come! Jesus has waited long enough. Don't try the Lord's patience."

The young Christians were now climbing up the fire escapes and kicking in windows. It looked as if it were a giant insect infestation. They were going into apartments and rousing people from their sleep, beating those who wouldn't come to Christ and carrying those who relented into a church.

Chulito looked down Manida Street and saw Martha fighting back. She had come out on her fire escape and kicked the Christians off as they climbed up. Martha made a sling out of her bra and was hurling cans of soup, tomato sauce, Vienna sausages—any canned good she had—to keep the Christians away.

Brenda was in the front window of her house with a high-heeled shoe in each hand and was swinging at the Christians climbing up the side of the house. "Take that, *carajo.*"

Kamikaze ran full speed down, dodging and shaking off Christians as if he were a pro football player. There was a sudden flash of metal and one of the "God is Awesome" guys hit Kamikaze in the back of his head. Kamikaze fell to the ground, rolled and got back up. "Get him!" the same "God is Awesome" man cried. A team of Christians charged toward Kamikaze from all sides of the street. He kicked them off, did a flip, and landed on the hood of a car. He pushed and punched and fought the

Christians. The man on the van, in between sobs, continued his rant, "Accept Jesus. He will give you a second chance. You don't have to live like this. Sin is like a cancer eating away at our society. Find true joy, Jesus will wait no more. Make a choice, brothers and sisters. There really is only one right decision and we have it right here." He held up a bible like Moses in *The Ten Commandments*.

Chulito saw Maria, Carlos's mother, shielding herself with a big lid from a pot in one hand and a frying pan in the other. Puti was suddenly dragged off to church. She was limp and exhausted from fighting. As they carried her, they stripped off her dress and heels, tossed them away, and dressed her, mid-air, in men's clothes. She was unconscious. Her mother, who never set foot in a church, trailed the mob, shouting, "Hallelujah!"

Chulito saw Carlos. He kicked and fought off his attackers. "Sodomite! Repent!" Carlos fought like a black belt martial arts expert. He made high kicks and deflected the swinging bibles. Chulito wanted to go to Carlos and fight with him, but he couldn't move.

The more Carlos, Kamikaze, Martha and Maria fought back, the more the Christians continued their attack, and called in for reinforcements.

The man with the bullhorn continued, "Don't fight it. Jesus is the way. Come to Jesus and you can end all the misery and strife. You don't have to fight. We offer a better life here on Earth and an eternal life with Christ in heaven. The choice is clear, my brothers and sisters—choose Christ or die. Yes! If you are not with Christ then your spirit is dead."

Kamikaze was tackled to the ground and a metal Bible crashed against his skull. A swarm had engulfed Martha's fire escape. Chulito saw Maria receive a blow that sent her to the ground and he called out, "No!"

A Christian heard the small voice in the locked car and looked at the tinted passenger seat window. A woman joined him and another person and another person and the car was quickly surrounded. They were tapping on the glass and looking in like zombies from a horror movie. "There's someone in there!" one of the women cried out, her hair pulled up in a tight bun. She had no makeup on. She came around to the front of the car where the windshield was not tinted. Chulito slipped down to the floor of the car. They rocked the car and slammed their bibles against it. Glass shattered. Then the woman with the tight bun leaned inside the car. She looked at Chulito eye-to-eye. "Do you accept Jesus as your personal savior?" The others kept tapping on the windows and shaking the car. Chulito couldn't speak. He heard Carlos calling out his name. There were people screaming and shouts of hallelujah in the air. "This is your chance. Tell me! Do you want forgiveness for all of your sins including the one you committed with Carlos the other night? God can wipe you clean. Do you accept him? Do you? Do you?" The others joined in, "Do you?! Do you?!" and continued tapping on the glass.

Chulito awoke with a jolt to Kamikaze tapping on the windshield of the car. "Hey Chulito, open the car, pana. My keys and remote are inside."

Chulito hit the switch. Kamikaze plopped into the car. "What happened, bro? You fell asleep and shit. Sorry I took so long—Brenda pulled an Eveready® and kept going and going and going," Kamikaze laughed. Chulito was still stunned from his dream. "Yo, what's the matter with you? You still asleep? And why you listening to this creepy music?"

The radio announcer said, "I hope you're enjoying the Enya Sunday morning music marathon..."

"No!" 'Kaze responded as he switched the station.

David Huberman

David Huberman was born in June 1956, somewhat anonymously, in a nameless Bronx hospital. He has a sister who works at Bellevue Hospital. He is an open-mic aficionado and has been published in *lungful magazine, Icon, Long Shot Magazine* and many of the *Unbearable* anthologies and lots of literary magazines.

Full Circle

Keeping to the shadows the man walked the streets, crossing the canals, his eyes scanning back and forth, making sure nobody noticed him. Noiseless, even in his movements, and sweating like a desperate animal, he didn't dare let panic take him over. Finally, he came to his destination. Staying very still in the early fog, the light rain wet his clothes. Crowds of people milled around, and for a second or two it felt like being at a carnival or a circus, but the red neon lights flickered brighter as the hours of dusk slowly disappeared. Soon night would come with the promise of a full moon and there would be no escape from its penetrating rays. There before him was Amsterdam's notorious red light district with its Turkish drug dealers mixing in with American senior citizens sightseeing on their special X-rated tours, gaunt junkies with sunken-in faces waiting, always waiting. Couples went into smoke shops with names like the Bob Marley Café or bars like the Red Dog with its pseudo-hippy or dreadlocks-Rasta atmosphere, where for a few gilders or American dollars you could score some nice blonde hashish, Colombian cannabis cakes, or drink any brand of beer brewed in Europe. There were the girls of course, partitioned off in small separate storefronts, sitting on stools, wearing—of course—the most amazing, exotic outfits. Through the windows, horny men of every nationality and age group gazed at them, fantasizing, judging, and haggling with their dream-girl.

The man spots the authorities and like that pop song from long ago, he watches the detectives. They seem to be very low-profile in this district, but then that's probably what they want criminals to think. Show yourself in a bar or a café and get spotted by one of their undercover agents and before you know it, like a predatory hawk that swoops down on a little mouse, you could be seized within its claws. That he couldn't afford, not now or ever. He had heard from a corrupt ex-Interpol agent that Scotland Yard and the other international law enforcement agencies had put his case-file on the back burner because of his age. He would be one-hundred and two years old, and whoever heard of a century-old man killing people? Yet wherever there were horrible murders, there lurked someone who looked a lot like Lawrence Talbot, and occasionally he would spot his old wanted poster being put back up again.

Unfortunately, he has no time to dwell on the authorities. Go with your plan, stay calm—and above all—don't panic, he told himself. Just then a group of men went by him; they were heading to patronize the "window" girls. He emerged from the fog and joined their group. They took no notice of him; their minds seemed to be on otherworldly problems. In less than two minutes, he found what he wanted. It wasn't the young woman that drew him in—rather it was her public comportment. Handcuffs!

Her place looked like a mini-medieval torture den. Larry pivots quickly just to make sure nobody is watching him as he enters. Before he can spit his words out the young temptress looks him in the eye and says, "Fifteen minutes, you know the score. One-hundred gilders." With his broad shoulders and dirty torn overcoat he came to rest on her stool. His wild greasy hair barely covered the map of wrinkles that etch his face, his red swollen eyes betray the fact that he hasn't slept for a long time. He gives her a weary smile, then says, "Pardon my appearance, but time is of the essence. I'll give you three-hundred British pounds—that's equal to six-hundred dollars in American money and about twelve-hundred gilders give or take. All I want you to do is handcuff me in the shackles over there, gag me, and then leave. You don't return until morning. You tell no one I'm here. My pounds are buying your silence, that's my deal. Please say yes."

With her Mediterranean features and hard body she eyed him intensely. "I don't do freaks." He wondered if she was Indonesian with her dark looks and coal-black hair. Maybe she's Arabic or gypsy, now that would be interesting. "No kinky stuff. This is Marlene's equipment; she works the day shift."

She doesn't seem to understand but somehow he must make her realize the stakes. "Look, if it's the money I'll double it! But we must hurry, for soon it'll be dark and then I change into...oh, it's so horrible!" He is close to breaking down.

Reluctantly she speaks. "Even he who is pure of heart and says his prayers by night can become a wolf when the wolf bane blooms and the autumn moon is bright."

Stunned silence follows.

"How did you..." Confusion trails his voice.

"My great-grandmother recited the poem to me when I was just a child. Maleva was her name. Dead a long time now, my gypsy clan honored her; said she had fought against the supernatural, but some great horror had befallen her. Funny, seeing you sitting there, reminded me of her. I hardly think of her anymore, and as for the poem, well I'm as surprised as you that I remember it. Who are you?"

Larry nods his head back and forth. "It's unbelievable, simply unbelievable. I've come full circle. Bela the gypsy was your grandfather! Then you must have heard of the curse, but it wasn't Maleva, rather her son upon whom the horror preyed." Fear had spread upon her young face, yet she did not try to leave. She said, "Bela's son Herman was my father! At the time of Bela's murder, no one in his clan had any knowledge that he was a young parent. Herman always said his father was killed by a rich Englishman. The murderer's name was Lawrence Talbot. Now I'll ask you again to tell me who you are!" she demanded.

With that question hanging from her lips, Larry got up from the stool, quietly approached her, and said gently, "I'm Lawrence Talbot. I was that fine British gentleman who killed your grandfather." He fully expected her to scream or to make a run for it, but she did neither. Softly, she said, "I want to hear everything."

Larry looked ahead of her, apprehension on his face. "Time is running out for words, but I'll say this: since the day of your grandfather's death I have been a fugitive, always on the run, scattering slaughtered men, women, and even children in my wake, but Bela I killed, I did not murder! Do you hear me child, I did this awful deed to defend myself when the mark of the beast was upon him and with his death I inherited your grandfather's curse; to never die, to live in eternal damnation—and every full moon to butcher another innocent human being! Good old Maleva, stood by her son and then later me, only she glimpsed into our hell and understood what it must have been like for us. And now the curse has come full circle, to deliver me to you, of all people, the great-granddaughter of the man who gave me the blasted curse of the Wolfman!

With those last words screaming upon his lips, Larry crumpled up and fell to his knees, moaning, crying, shrieking the words "Why me God, why me?" His listener came to him with compassion on her face, lightly stroking his unkempt hair. It was as if he were a small child and she the Earth Mother, the goddess, the all-knowing spiritual teacher. As she caressed him, Larry grabbed her hand and saw there scarred in the middle of her palm the sign of the pentagram. This was a certain sign of his next victim! With utter shock he jumped up, "Too late!" He cried out.

Through the cheap curtains, as moonlight flooded the room, he instantly felt the changes coursing through his body. Gobs of drool dripped from his mouth; his teeth enlarged, bigger and sharper, and became fangs that grew down to his chin. Each body hair stood up, growing at a super-accelerated rate, transforming him from human to beast. Larry's last memory was of a wolf howling at the moon, then of attacking, ripping, tearing, biting—trapped in a total bloodlust until darkness descended.

He woke with a start, the sunlight dancing before him. The birds were singing, but not to him. He threw himself from the bed, naked, in a panic, exactly like a hundred times before. The small room was in disarray, cold cream on the floor, the shackles torn down—handcuffs torn into pieces of useless metal. As he moved, he felt pain across his body. There in front of the smashed mirror, he examined his naked torso. To his great astonishment, there were huge welts and scratches all over his body. The poor girl, she must have put up an awful fight, he thought, but where is her body? Within his horror of finding his hideous handiwork, he examined the room for her torn-up corpse. No body! Not even small amounts of blood! Impossible, could she have escaped me?

No, it can't be. Once I see the symbol of the pentagram, my victims are as good as dead. No one has ever escaped my attack. No one!

Then came a knock on the door. A bewildered Larry stood transfixed as he heard her husky voice. "Oh Larry, it's me. I'm coming in. I have coffee. I didn't know how you like it so I got..." The gypsy girl casually walked in. Seeing her, Larry stared and said in total amazement, "But...but...you're alive!" She walked over to him slowly, put the coffee down on the broken dresser, and kissed him long and hard on the mouth. He jumped away from her in fear. He was startled, nearly out of his mind. She looked at him seductively and said, "Lawrence, you didn't kill anybody last night. Sit down, Larry, we have to talk."

He was dumbfounded. "What happened last night?" he asked. Was it possible that for the first time he had not killed a victim chosen for him by the vision of the pentagram? Shocking, simply shocking, he mused, as the thought hit him like a sledgehammer.

She woke him from this daydream. "Mating, that's your answer. That's what will stop the needless killing. It can be quite as violent as murdering someone, lovemaking at its most furious! It's our solution, Larry, yours and mine together." Confused by her remarks, he was at a loss for words.

"Oh Lawrence," she said, her voice as shy as a little girl. "I turn just like you do. Did you think only men bear the curse of the wolf? I know very well the feeling of waking in a sticky, bloody pool of an evening's unlucky prey." She stopped speaking. There was no further need of words. They looked at each other, as two fierce animals wildly sniffing a compatible creature's scent. "Your clothes are on the chair, over there where you hung from the shackles last night. That is, before you tore them down." Wordlessly, he dressed as fast as possible. He was numb with this new awareness. Had he found the solution at last? Finally he was ready to leave.

As he departed, her last words were reflected in her piercing gypsy eyes. "Lawrence, my love—stay hidden, but don't go too far. Come back to me before the next full moon. Remember Larry, mating. It's our way now, our beautiful way."

*** FIN ***

Made in the USA
Charleston, SC
22 December 2010